THE LMS GUIDE BOOK

LEARNING MANAGEMENT SYSTEMS DEMYSTIFIED

STEVEN D. FOREMAN

atd PRESS

25 24 23 22 3 4 5 6

ATD Press is an internationally renowned source of insightful and practical information on talent development, workplace learning, and professional development.

ATD Press
1640 King Street
Alexandria, VA 22314 USA

Ordering information: Books published by ATD Press can be purchased by visiting ATD's website at www.td.org/books or by calling 800.628.2783 or 703.683.8100.

Library of Congress Control Number: 2017956602

ISBN-10: 1-60728-309-3
ISBN-13: 978-1-60728-309-6
e-ISBN: 978-1-60728-165-8

ATD Press Editorial Staff
Director: Kristine Luecker
Manager: Melissa Jones
Community of Practice Manager, Learning Technologies: Justin Brusino
Developmental Editor: Jack Harlow
Senior Associate Editor: Caroline Coppel
Cover Design: Derek Thornton, Faceout Studio
Text Design: Francelyn Fernandez
Printed by BR Printers, San Jose, CA

To my Dad

David C. Foreman

1928-2017

Contents

Foreword

> "You must choose, but choose wisely, for as the true Grail will bring you life, a false one will take it from you."
>
> —*The Grail Knight to Indiana Jones in* Indiana Jones and the Last Crusade *(1989)*

While choosing and implementing a learning management system (LMS) is certainly not a life or death situation, your decisions and actions along the way (and the consequences) often make the process seem like one. LMS selection, implementation, and management are tough jobs. Choosing wisely, based on knowledge, experience, and proven practices, can go a long way toward avoiding an LMS experience that could be almost as bad as drinking from the wrong Grail.

But that's easier said than done. As a speaker at many e-learning conferences and corporate meetings, I usually ask my audience if they have an LMS. Almost all raise their hands. I then ask how many are on their second LMS. More than half the hands are still in the air. When I get to a third or fourth LMS, and there are quite a few hands still raised, I start to wonder why there's so much churn in LMS purchases. The reasons, of course, are varied, but over the years, a common thread has become clear:

"We bought before we thought."

There is no doubt that the LMS world is fraught with challenges and tough decisions. After all, you can spend a boatload of money on the software, and then another boatload on implementation. You don't just need savvy in LMS technologies; you also need to build support for your LMS investment.

When seeking an LMS, you need to get three things right. First, you need an overall learning strategy that the LMS can support. The LMS itself is not a strategy, but it can be a good strategy enabler. Then, you need to select the right LMS for your organization—not just for today's needs, but for future ones as well. Buying an LMS can be a bumpy road—and a very expensive one—or it can be an easy, well-paved superhighway. And finally, you can't just get an LMS and declare victory; you need to implement it correctly. Turning on an LMS without careful consideration of how it will be used can spell disaster.

Steve Foreman, a leader in LMS strategy, selection, and implementation, tackles the process head-on. After dozens of soup-to-nuts LMS projects in large corporations, small businesses, and government agencies, he knows a thing or two not just about LMS products and technologies, but also about the value that a solid LMS can bring to a training department and the organization as a whole.

Steve brings his experience to bear in a clear set of steps to acquire and implement an LMS. For trainers and their managers, the book provides a pathway for making sure the selected LMS is the right one and implemented correctly. For IT professionals, the book details some of the major technical issues that must be addressed for the LMS to fulfill its mission. For senior managers, the book represents best practices in LMS acquisition and implementation that can improve effectiveness and save money by doing it right the first time.

And do not fear: This book is not LMS hype. Steve does not tout one LMS over another or push you to rush into buying a certain LMS type. He has seen enough LMS mistakes to know that not every organization needs the same things from an LMS—and some might not need one at all. Every LMS selection and implementation is unique to the organization doing the project. This is not a cookbook either, but you should consider all the ideas in *The LMS Guidebook* for a successful project.

Steve takes a realistic look at LMS initiatives—the good and the bad—to come up with recommendations for making it all work. Even if this is your second or third LMS, you will likely find information and checkpoints that you weren't aware of that will help you do a better job this time.

The book has lots of technical information and LMS jargon, some intended for trainers and some for IT professionals. There is no way a successful LMS project can work without addressing some serious technology issues, so Steve doesn't shy away from any of them. That's why the included glossary is so robust.

If this is your first LMS selection and implementation project, it's probably a bigger undertaking than you first realized, but this book can help you make the right decisions, the first time. If you've been through this before, you still probably don't know where all the pitfalls are, but you have certainly gained a healthy respect for them. *The LMS Guidebook* can help you avoid the mistakes of the past.

Like all software and software vendors, the LMS market is in a constant state of flux. New players replace (or merge with) old, technologies evolve, and organizations find new uses for their LMS while, at the same time, getting rid of some of the old uses. If you think this is going to be simple, think again. And start planning. An LMS is a big-time IT investment, and you will have a lot riding on this.

You will need to skirt some land mines on your LMS journey, but the destination is a host of great opportunities for your organization and the learners you serve. Steve knows the best route and is marking the trail. Now all you have to do is follow it.

Marc Rosenberg, PhD
Hillsborough, New Jersey
December 2017

Acknowledgments

Much of what I've learned throughout my career has resulted from collaboration with smart, creative, and talented people. In particular, I want to acknowledge four colleagues from whom I have learned so much over the years. Thank you, Marc Rosenberg, John Larson, Alan Cohen, and Rob Davis.

Thanks to Lisa Mattson and Sandra DeCastro at IMS Global® for providing information related to the LTI®, QTI®, OneRoster®, Common Cartridge®, Thin Common Cartridge®, Caliper Analytics®, and Open Badges specifications.

Thanks to Andy Johnson, Jason Haag, Robby Robson, and Peter Berking at ADL, as well as the cmi5 Working Group, for providing information on the total learning architecture and the xAPI, cmi5, and CASS specifications.

And now a walk down memory lane to acknowledge the InfoMedia Designs team of the mid- to late 1990s, who worked with me to develop a very early web-based learning management system for a multinational communications company. Our LMS was focused on supporting what would eventually become known as blended learning programs. Complementary solutions included a socially adaptive knowledge base and online communities of practice. Together, these platforms provided technology and process support for an early learning and performance ecosystem. Thanks to Rob Davis, Carl Chase, Bill Weisbach, Rick Ziminski, Alan Zeldin, Dean DesRosiers, Jackie Figueroa, Vanessa Fox, Alon Baram, Stephen Dempsey, and John Larson for all that innovative work. You were ahead of your time.

Thanks to all the InfoMedia Designs customers who have hired us over the years to assist in evaluating and selecting, implementing and integrating, and optimizing and improving operations for their LMS.

Many thanks to Justin Brusino, Jack Harlow, Caroline Coppel, and all the other hardworking folks at ATD, who helped bring this book to fruition.

Additional thanks to my longtime friend and colleague Marc Rosenberg for providing valuable guidance, suggestions, and edits.

And a very special note of thanks to Patti Shank, who first suggested I write this book and put me in touch with Justin and ATD.

Introduction

Just a few years after Tim Berners Lee invented it, the World Wide Web became ubiquitous in our daily lives and made many new applications of networked computer technology possible. One of these technologies, the learning management system (LMS), has been a staple in business, academia, and government since the mid-1990s. Over the last decade, advances in technology, changing workforce demographics, and the emergence of instructional design models that are more social, experiential, adaptive, and gamified have raised the question, is the LMS is still relevant?

Over the years, I have read many articles and blog posts declaring the imminent death of the LMS. The usual argument is that the LMS has not kept up with the times in which we find ourselves, when people are learning informally through social networks, knowledge bases, games, and short microlearning videos. And yet why are so many LMS products available, and why do so many organizations still have or want one? In fact, a 2016 study by MarketsandMarkets estimated the LMS market to have been worth $5.22 billion in 2016 and forecasts that it will grow to $15.72 billion by 2021. The bottom line is this: As long as organizations need to deliver courses, LMS products will continue to exist as an option.

Despite the proliferation of LMS products, there is still a good deal of confusion about what they actually do. When I ask people what LMS their organization uses, the responses I get are sometimes unexpected. I have heard people equate an LMS with e-learning authoring tools, web-conferencing systems, and social networking platforms. Clearly, there is some misunderstanding about what an LMS is, what it does, and what is involved in acquiring and operating one, not to mention getting a return on your investment. One of my goals in writing this book is to address this confusion.

I have also come across a great deal of customer dissatisfaction with LMS products. Some of my most popular conference presentations and workshops have had titles like Pain in the LMS and Avoiding an L-M-Mess. Over time, I have found several reasons for this dissatisfaction. One is customers who are unhappy with their LMS vendor's level of responsiveness or lack of alignment with their priorities for new product features. Another stems from problems with a product's usability, including its look and feel, complexity, or inadequate searching and reporting capabilities. Yet another is a result of the customer's lack of diligence in defining requirements and evaluating the right products for the right reasons, leaving them with a product that is not well suited to their needs. Last is the customer's lack of governance, standards, and processes, which results in a mix of outdated and poorly defined content that makes their LMS hard to use.

Putting a new LMS in place involves a significant investment in money, time, and resources and can be very disruptive to the L&D function and the organization as a whole. *The LMS Guidebook* is intended to help organizations minimize the disruption and get the most value from their investment by clearing up the confusion about the LMS and providing a set of proven practices for how to go about evaluating, selecting, implementing, and operating an LMS.

Why This Book?

The LMS Guidebook offers a broad view of the LMS industry and its various product categories. It offers guidance on how to go about evaluating and selecting an LMS. This shouldn't come as a surprise, but not all LMS products are the same—they won't all meet your needs. One of the purposes of this book is to enable you to ask better questions of vendors about their products and evaluate those products in a way that improves your decision-making process and increases your likelihood of successful software selection and implementation.

Once you have found the right LMS, you will be embarking on a potentially large-scale implementation project. This book offers in-depth guidance on LMS implementation and operation. It provides the information you need to effectively plan and execute all aspects of your LMS implementation, including how to establish appropriate standards, processes, and governance, and collaborate effectively with the IT function to ensure that the LMS works within your technology infrastructure.

Additionally, *The LMS Guidebook* covers the industry standards and specifications relevant to LMS products, and provides a glimpse of the future role of the LMS in the broader learning and performance ecosystem.

Who This Book Is For

If you are on the technical side of the LMS, there are many terms and concepts in this book that you'll already know and that may seem overexplained. Hopefully, you will find value in the book's description of LMS use models, processes, standards, and approaches, as well as how technology decisions play into LMS selection and implementation activities.

If you are on the instructional side of the LMS, you may find unfamiliar technical terms and concepts. I have done my best to explain the technology and added two glossaries at the end of the book, which you may find helpful. The first is a glossary of IT technical jargon. The second is a glossary of terms that have different meanings for L&D and IT. If you are able to talk about LMS technology with your IT partners, both parties are likely to emerge from those discussions with a more unified approach and a healthy working relationship.

But no matter your technical or instructional competencies, to get the most out of *The LMS Guidebook,* you should have a basic understanding of the L&D world and its lexicon. This involves courses, classes, curricula, credits, certification, compliance, course completion certificates, and other words that start with *c*—and relevant terms and concepts that start with other letters, too.

How This Book Is Organized

The book is split into three parts. Part 1, "What an LMS Does and How It Works," contains the first five chapters. Chapters 1-4 provide a thorough grounding in the LMS market, the types of LMS products available, and the features you should expect to see in each type of LMS product. Chapter 5 delves into the various LMS-related industry and de facto standards of which you should be aware.

Part 2, "How to Select, Implement, and Operate an LMS," has five chapters. The first, chapter 6, provides a clear set of steps to follow for evaluating products and selecting a new LMS. Chapters 7-9 provide detailed guidance on all the tasks required for effective LMS implementation. Chapter 10 focuses on how to operate your LMS efficiently—an area that is often overlooked by organizations and can lead directly to user dissatisfaction, poor data quality, and a negative perception of the LMS.

Part 3, "Beyond the LMS," has two chapters. Chapter 11 discusses how LMS solutions are evolving to keep up with current and future needs. Chapter 12 concludes the book by introducing the concept of a broader learning and performance ecosystem, a more comprehensive learning strategy that many organizations are moving toward, and how the LMS fits into this bigger picture.

Key takeaways are listed at the end of each chapter and included in appendix A, forming a comprehensive list of the most important considerations for your LMS project. The glossary of IT technical jargon in appendix B defines technical terms you will hear from vendors and your IT staff as you work on implementing your LMS. This is followed by a second, shorter glossary in appendix C, which contains a few terms that have different meanings for L&D and IT. You must take precautions when using these terms with your IT partners. I have seen situations where everyone was using the same term thinking they understood one another, while they were actually talking past one another because of the different meanings of the terms.

How to Read This Book

The LMS Guidebook will not tell you which LMS product you should buy. No book can do that because each organization—its needs and its resources—is different, and because the LMS market is crowded with so many vendors and products of different sizes, features, complexities, and costs. Matching the right LMS to the right organizational need is as much a function of experience and insight as it is about process and technology.

But this book does provide a comprehensive set of proven practices for LMS selection, implementation, and operation. It will help you get organized and put you on the right path to success. It will enable you and your team to manage a lot of issues, obstacles, and opportunities of which you may not have been aware. Share it with everyone who has a stake in your LMS project—or better yet, buy one for each member on the team.

Finally, this book reflects my experiences with many clients who have successfully selected and launched an LMS, and with others who have upgraded or replaced an existing LMS. While confidentiality rules limit my discussion of specific clients, the lessons learned and proven practices that came out of this work have greatly influenced the pages that follow.

Your LMS journey will be challenging, but I have found that it can be a satisfying one. It can also be a great learning experience, resulting in an outcome that provides value to you and your organization.

Good luck with your LMS initiatives!

PART 1

What an LMS Does and How It Works

CHAPTER 1

What Is a Learning Management System?

This chapter defines *learning management system* and describes the three main types of LMS products. It identifies the key advantages of commercial and open source products and lists the costs associated with acquiring an LMS. It describes stand-alone LMS products and those packaged as apps or plug-ins to popular software frameworks. It also compares an LMS with a learning record store.

A learning management system (LMS) is not the remedy for all your organization's learning challenges. But it can be useful, especially to organizations that provide training and education programs to employees, customers, suppliers, distributors, professional association members, military personnel, college students, and others. If your organization is one of these, you probably know that managing the delivery of learning programs presents many challenges.

Training events such as classes, workshops, and seminars must be scheduled for a specific time and place. The event may be at a physical location or a web address, as in the case of a webinar or virtual class. People must be able to enroll in the training event, and one or more instructors must be assigned to deliver the training program, take attendance, and issue credit for course completion.

Self-paced training introduces its own set of challenges. Course software and other digital materials must be uploaded and published for online access. People must be able to locate and launch the course. Their work must be tracked and recorded automatically so that they can receive credit. People who exit before finishing the course must be able to resume at the point they left off.

And of course, some training requires a blend of scheduled events, self-paced modules, assignments, tests, surveys, and other components.

Clearly, the need to manage and track training programs of all types requires software that can handle the task with sophistication and ease, and provide the L&D function with information it needs to improve its services to individual learners and the organization as a whole. An LMS can contribute significantly to this goal.

LMS Explained

Before going any further, we need to establish what an LMS is. Let's start with a basic definition:

> An LMS is a multiuser software application, usually accessed through a web browser. It helps organizations manage training events, self-paced courses, and blended learning programs. It provides automation that replaces rigorous and expensive manual work, saves time, and enables you to organize your content, data, and learners. It tracks and reports on training activity and results.

If the key word in your organization's name is *education, training, learning, performance,* or some combination of them, you probably need an LMS. However, there are several different types out there. The specific type you need depends on what you are trying to accomplish.

3 Types of LMS Products

If you are confused about what an LMS is and what it does, you are not alone. Even if you believe you have a clear understanding, you may be surprised to learn that there are three distinctly different types of LMS, each with its own unique feature set. The learning management capabilities you need may be found in one or more of these product categories.

I have worked with organizations that started out trying to compare products from two or all three of these categories. After much wheel spinning and head scratching, they discovered that they were comparing apples with oranges. If you are getting ready to buy an LMS and don't have a basic understanding of the LMS landscape, you may waste valuable time and effort evaluating products that are not optimally suited to your organization's needs. So let's take a quick look at the LMS marketplace.

I find it helpful to break down LMS products into three major categories, which I call corporate LMS, academic LMS, and integrated LCMS-LMS (the *C* in *LCMS* stands for content). While these labels are generally not used by vendors, they can help you understand the LMS business and make better LMS choices. But be careful not to rule out any of these categories because of its label. For example, many corporations use academic LMS products instead of, or in addition to, a corporate LMS. The labels are more about *how* each type of LMS is used rather than *who* uses it. Ultimately, a better understanding of these categories may help you focus on the type of product that best meets your needs.

Corporate LMS

A corporate LMS is about connecting people with learning programs. It has a catalog of all the courses you offer. People log in to the corporate LMS to register and get credit for your courses.

Corporate LMS products are primarily geared toward organizations that offer relatively short courses that may range from an hour or less to several days. They typically contain courses that a company's employees might need related to sales, customer service, products, policies and procedures, soft skills, personal productivity, management and leadership, new hire orientation, regulatory compliance, and other relevant topics.

Most LMS products are in this category, and there are many corporate LMS products available.

Academic LMS

An academic LMS is an online extension of, or replacement for, the classroom. It is a website where instructors and students meet and collaborate online. Instructors can post materials and assignments. Students can chat with the instructor or with one another, hand in assignments, and take quizzes.

Academic LMS products are primarily geared toward institutions that offer courses spanning a term or semester. There are a few dozen academic LMS products available.

Integrated LCMS-LMS

An integrated LCMS-LMS provides many of the same course delivery features as a corporate LMS. But it also offers features not found in a corporate LMS for developing, or authoring, content. Many course developers use PC or Mac authoring tool software to create online courses. Others use an LCMS to create not just online courses, but also job aids, instructor and student guides, and other types of learning content. Some of the most robust LCMS products are strictly focused on content development and do not offer any of the LMS capabilities needed to deliver the content to learners. But a growing number of products now offer both content creation and delivery capabilities. I call this type of hybrid product an integrated LCMS-LMS.

> A learning content management system (LCMS) is a collaborative content development environment for course developers. It has a searchable library that stores and organizes digital source materials. Developers can check items out of the library to work on them and check them back in when finished. Workflows are established to manage the content development pipeline and notify developers, editors, and reviewers of actions they need to take. Templates can be created and used to make the appearance of content uniform.

Using More Than 1 Type of LMS

Some organizations use more than one type of LMS. For example, an organization may use a corporate LMS to manage self-registration, provide access to web-based courses, schedule training events, and track and report on training activity. The same organization may use an academic LMS for its virtual classes.

Commercial Versus Open Source LMS Products

Beyond the three types of LMS products already covered, both commercial and open source products are available. The key advantage of a commercial LMS is that it is fully supported by the manufacturer. If you run into problems, you have someone to call for help. The key advantage of an open source LMS is that there are no licensing costs. If you are on a tight budget, this is worth serious consideration.

Table 1-1 compares commercial and open source in terms of who owns the product, how product enhancements are managed, how costs are structured, and how the product is supported.

If you are unfamiliar with some of the technical terms, please refer to appendix B for a glossary of IT technical jargon.

Table 1-1. Commercial Versus Open Source LMS Products

	Commercial	**Open Source**
Product Ownership	The manufacturer retains sole control of product features, functionality, releases, and upgrades.	A voluntary community of software developers collaborates to develop, test, and release new product features and bug fixes.
Product Enhancements	• Customers may request new features. The manufacturer decides whether and when to add the requested features to its product development road map. Typically, features being requested by multiple customers get the most attention. • When a new version of the product is released, all the manufacturer's customers are able to take advantage of the new features.	• Organizations using the product may document a need for new features. The community agrees on which new features to build into the product. • Product source code is available and can be modified by anyone with software development skills; however, changes made without the consent of the community do not get incorporated into the official product.
Product Costs	• Annual or monthly licensing fees are typically charged to use the product, often on a cost-per-user basis that may be fixed or may decrease with more users. • Annual or monthly hosting, maintenance, and support fees may be charged separately or built into the licensing costs.	• There are no licensing costs. • Organizations and individuals can freely download the software, but must make their own arrangements for product hosting, installation, and maintenance.

Table 1-1. Commercial Versus Open Source LMS Products (cont.)

	Commercial	Open Source
Product Costs (cont.)	• Hosting fees typically cover a production environment that users can access. Additional fees may be charged for more environments, such as a staging instance of the LMS, where administrators can test new releases, integrations, and configuration changes before they are installed in the production environment. • One-time set-up fees may be charged for product installation and administrator training. • Some manufacturers also provide professional services on a time-and-materials or fixed-price basis to customers who need help with data migration from legacy systems or systems integrations.	
Product Support	• Manufacturers typically offer support plans and options, which define how to contact support staff, how trouble tickets are prioritized and resolved, hours of operation, typical turnaround timeframes, and issue escalation procedures. • Manufacturers may offer support service guarantees such as average bug report response time and average resolution time for bugs at each priority level.	• Open source community members often post blogs and online discussions to address product questions and issues. • Some third-party vendors may offer commercial hosting and support services for specific open source products.

Stand-Alone LMS Products

Most LMS products are offered as a complete, stand-alone system. In other words, the LMS has its own web address and user interface. Many of these products have administrator-configurable properties that enable you to implement your own branding, logo, and color scheme. You can enable the features you want to use and disable those you do not. For example, if you want to require that people pay to take your courses, you could turn on the product's e-commerce features. However, if your courses are intended for employees, you could disable e-commerce.

These products usually offer integration capabilities that allow the LMS to share user account information and training data with other systems, such as human resource management systems (HRMS) used by businesses, membership management systems (MMS) used by professional associations, and student information systems (SIS) used by academic institutions. This is important because it improves the integrity of your data. If your LMS does not share user account data with your HRMS, MMS, or SIS, then user accounts must be created from scratch in the LMS. This can lead to discrepancies where the LMS user profile data differ from the data in your other systems, leaving you to wonder which system is correct.

Just a few years ago, all LMS products were stand-alone systems, and they still dominate the LMS market. In recent years, however, LMS products have emerged in the form of apps and plug-ins, which deserve some attention.

LMS Apps and Plug-Ins

A growing number of LMS products are available as apps and plug-ins that add learning management features to your existing website. If your organization's website is built atop a popular software framework such as WordPress, Salesforce, or Microsoft SharePoint, you should consider an LMS app or plug-in.

Like stand-alone LMS products, LMS apps and plug-ins can be commercial or open source and may offer corporate, academic, or LCMS-LMS feature sets. They generally provide the same functionality as their stand-alone cousins.

Because LMS apps and plug-ins are seamlessly embedded in your website, the user experience is more consistent and streamlined. People can access your courses without leaving your site to go to a separate system. This means that your customers or professional association members can view and purchase courses alongside other products and services, your employees can access learning programs alongside related documents and other content, and your academic students can access their courses through your student portal.

LMS apps and plug-ins are integrated with the data in your WordPress, Salesforce, or SharePoint framework. The same user database employed by other features of your website is also utilized by the LMS, and your LMS data are accessed through the framework's reporting tool.

- WordPress can be extended using plug-ins. Adding an LMS plug-in to WordPress allows you to add course delivery and reporting capabilities while you maintain control of the overall look, feel, and layout of your website.
- Salesforce refers to their extensions as apps. Adding an LMS app to Salesforce enables you to offer product training to your customers, sell courses side by side with your other products and services, or train sales and customer service representatives.
- SharePoint also allows for apps. By adding an LMS app to SharePoint, you can introduce learning management functionality to your website and integrate your courses with SharePoint's content management and social networking capabilities for a blended learning experience.

LMS Versus Learning Record Store

There is another learning technology called a learning record store (LRS), which is associated with the Experience API (xAPI) specification. (Read more about what you can do with xAPI and learning record stores in chapter 5.) But what is the difference between an LMS and an LRS? Should you get an LMS or an LRS?

The purpose of an LMS is to help you schedule, distribute, and manage the delivery of learning programs and provide direct access to people who use those programs. LMS users are learners, instructors, and learning administrators.

In contrast, the purpose of an LRS is to store the xAPI learning activity data generated by your websites, systems, and applications. LRS users are xAPI developers and data analysts.

Some LMS products that support xAPI have a built-in LRS or can connect to a third-party LRS. Increasingly, organizations are using an LMS to manage their formal learning programs and xAPI and an LRS to collect data on the informal learning that happens through social networks, knowledge bases, performance support systems, instructional games and simulations, and elsewhere.

Key Takeaways

This chapter introduced three types of LMS products (corporate, academic, and LCMS-LMS); compared the pros and cons of commercial versus open source products; discussed how an LMS can be a stand-alone product or an app or plug-in; and explained the key differences between an LMS and an LRS. If you plan to acquire the appropriate LMS solution for your organization, you need to understand the choices available. The key takeaways are:

- An LMS is a multiuser software application, usually accessed through a web browser, that helps organizations manage training events, self-paced courses, and blended learning programs.
- The three main categories of LMS products are corporate LMS, academic LMS, and integrated LCMS-LMS. Each has a unique feature set and use model.
- There are commercial and open-source LMS products. A commercial LMS is fully supported by the manufacturer; an open source LMS has no licensing costs.
- Most LMS products are stand-alone systems. However, some are packaged as apps or plug-ins for popular website frameworks such as WordPress, SharePoint, and Salesforce.
- An LMS should not be confused with an LRS, which collects and stores xAPI learning data generated in other systems. While LMS users are learners, instructors, and learning administrators, LRS users are xAPI developers and data analysts.

Now that you have a basic understanding of what an LMS is and is not, chapters 2-4 will delve more deeply into the features available in corporate LMS products, academic LMS products, and LCMS-LMS products, respectively.

CHAPTER 2

Corporate LMS Features

This chapter goes into more detail about what a corporate LMS is. It describes features of a corporate LMS that allow you to manage users and courses, track user-course interactions, administer the system, and run reports. It also covers extra features you might find in some corporate LMS products for social networking, extending training to customers and business partners, and managing competencies and talent.

If you are not sure which type of LMS is right for your organization, a deeper explanation of the features available in each type of product will help. This chapter explores the features of the corporate LMS.

Organizations use a corporate LMS to deliver learning programs, most often to employees and, in some cases, to customers and business partners. Of the hundreds of commercial LMS products available, most fall squarely in this category. Corporate LMS products offer some of the most robust features and functionality. A corporate LMS contains user accounts and instructional content. It handles transactions between users and content and keeps track of the data generated when people use content.

Corporate LMS administrators can create and configure web-based and instructor-led programs; manage class schedules; manage resources like classrooms, equipment, and instructors;

view rosters; track attendance, scores, and progress; run reports; and perform a variety of other tasks. Corporate LMS learners can browse and search course catalogs, register for classes, launch web-based programs, receive email notifications, earn credits, and view a transcript.

Let's say you work for a multinational corporation. Your employees work in four global regions. Your company's products, services, and business processes vary from region to region, as do the native languages spoken by employees and the regulatory compliance requirements. At the same time, your company's values, HR policies, quality assurance practices, and many other topics must be consistent in all regions. How will you ensure the right people get the right training? You can use a corporate LMS to deliver global and region-specific training, whether it is e-learning, classroom based, or blended. You can assign global and regional LMS administrators to manage their own content. You can deploy courses in the appropriate languages to the appropriate regions. And you can track and report on your fulfillment of regulatory compliance requirements around the globe. These are just a few examples of what your company can do with a corporate LMS.

A corporate LMS targets business organizations as its primary customers, but it may also be used in government, professional association, or academic settings. The core features of a corporate LMS can be organized into the categories of user management, course management, user-course transactions, administration, and reporting. The following sections will delve into these core feature sets.

User Management Features

A corporate LMS must support the creation and maintenance of user accounts. Users must be able to log in to their accounts through a process called authentication. A user profile contains important information about each user. Users can be associated with the job roles and organizations in which they work. User groups or audiences can be created that enable you to connect the right people with the most relevant learning programs.

User Accounts

A user account must contain a unique user ID, username, and password. The user ID may be a system-generated number, an employee ID, or some other convention. What is important is that each user has an identifier that differentiates them from every other user in the system.

Typically, organizations set up the LMS to share user information with another system that already contains accounts for the same people who will use the LMS, like a human resource management system, member management system, or student information system. For organizations that don't have one of these systems, the LMS can be configured to allow administrators to create user accounts manually or for users to create their own user accounts.

When you allow users to create their own accounts, people often forget their login information and simply create another account. These duplicate accounts may have incomplete and conflicting information. And while many LMS products allow you to merge duplicate accounts by combining the user profiles and training records for two user accounts, it can be difficult for administrators to notice when duplicate accounts exist. For these reasons and others, many organizations disable the ability for users to create or change their own accounts and, instead, import user accounts and profile data from a source system, such as a corporation's human resource management system or a professional organization's member management system.

Because users and their user profile data are constantly changing, importing the data once is not enough. The LMS user data must be synchronized with the source system so that, when the source data change, the change is replicated in the LMS. This typically involves a recurring scheduled process, such as a nightly feed of the data to the LMS.

Authentication

Authentication is the process through which an LMS identifies a user from the credentials they used to log in, authorizes them to use the system, and matches them to the appropriate user account. LMS systems always perform authentication when a user logs in, as do many other corporate systems and commercial websites.

If you've ever had to remember your login credentials for multiple systems and log in and out of systems you use throughout the day, you'll appreciate single sign-on (SSO). Essentially, SSO allows your users to log in to your network or corporate portal once, and then gain access to other systems (including your LMS) without needing to log in again. This is possible because the credentials they used to log in to the network or portal are authenticated once, and then passed behind the scenes to all other systems they use throughout the day. Most LMS products support a variety of popular SSO methods.

> Single sign-on (SSO) is a method for maintaining the identity of users in a central repository, sometimes called an identity provider, which is available to multiple enterprise systems and applications. After the user has logged in to one of the systems, they are then automatically logged in to any other SSO-enabled system they access on the network.

User Profiles

A user profile is a collection of data that describe the user. It may include the user's name (prefix, first, middle, last, suffix); contact information (email address, work or home address, phone numbers); employment information (position title, level, hire date, manager's user ID); demographics (gender, birth date, preferred language); and other pertinent information.

These data are important to support a variety of features in the LMS. For example, the LMS might use the user's name and email address to send reminders and transaction confirmation messages. Associating users with their manager allows managers to approve training registration requests if needed or otherwise participate in the users' learning. You can also target a new employee orientation course to people with a recent hire date or highlight courses available in the user's preferred language.

Job Roles and Organizations

Many corporate LMS products support the management of a list of job roles and your organizational structure. Although we have been using the term *organization* in reference to the larger enterprise, the LMS uses the term to refer to any node in your organizational hierarchy, which might include, for example, business units, departments, divisions, and districts. Each of these is considered an organization in the LMS, and the reporting relationships between these organizations reflect your organizational hierarchy.

Job roles and organization structures are often imported from another system, like an HRMS. Each user can be associated with a job role and a node in the organizational structure. This allows administrators to target training and generate reports for users in a specific job or organization.

For example, you can use LMS organization data to assign training or generate a report for a single organization and all organizations underneath it in the hierarchy. Let's say your company is organized with the sales divisions for all product lines reporting to a single executive; you can run a report on that executive's entire organization, or any part of it. LMS job role data add another dimension to LMS reports. If you want to look specifically at the account managers in the sales organization, you can add the account manager job role to your report's parameters to further refine your results.

User Groups or Audiences

Many corporate LMS products provide a way for authorized administrators to create any number of user groups or audiences by selecting specific user profile, job role, and organization fields or using them in combination. This allows you to target courses for learners who have completed a specific prerequisite, reside in a specific geographical location, or speak a specific language.

A few LMS products provide a robust method for defining user groups using operators such as *and, or,* and *not.* For example, a user group may be configured to comprise all LMS users who manage direct reports *and* whose job role is account manager *or* sales manager *or* regional sales manager *and* whose hire date is less than three months prior to the current date, but *not* those who have already completed the course New Sales Manager Orientation. Once you have defined a user group, you can use it to assign specific training or run targeted reports.

Role-Based Views

Role-based views make it possible for users to see their own view of the content in an LMS, which is tailored to their user profile, job role, and organization. For example, an IT systems administrator may search or browse for a course on customer relationship management (CRM) and find a list of courses on CRM systems and systems administration. A customer service agent may search or browse on the same topic and find a list of courses on customer service features, processes, incident reporting, and key performance indicators. A salesperson perusing the same topic may find courses on customer sales history features, customer intelligence reporting, customer touchpoints, and marketing programs.

You can enable role-based views by restricting the visibility of a course to one or more user groups. The benefit to users is that irrelevant courses are removed from view, improving the system's usability and reducing the risk of signing up for the wrong course.

Course Management Features

A corporate LMS contains a catalog of all your organization's course offerings. Courses may be self-paced or event-based with a location, instructor, and start and end date. Each course has a title, description, and other properties such as prerequisites, credits, and completion certificates. Courses may be structured in a variety of ways with any combination and sequence of tutorials, assignments, surveys, and tests.

Course Catalog

A course catalog is a directory of the learning programs available in the LMS. Each course has a collection of properties, including, but not limited to, course title, code, description, and credits. People can search or browse the course catalog.

Searching the Catalog

LMS search capabilities can be somewhat limited when compared with the web search tools that we are accustomed to using. An LMS typically requires the user to enter search terms with exact spelling and capitalization to find matching courses. Often, the system only searches by course title and course code; some systems also search the course description.

Browsing the Catalog

People who want to explore the course catalog can do so with a calendar or list view, or both. The calendar view shows course offerings on the dates they are scheduled to begin and end. The list view may be menu driven—allowing people to browse topics of interest in the menu, select a topic, and see a list of courses—or a complete listing of all courses that can be shortened by selecting a topic, delivery method, or other filters from drop-down lists. You can define your own catalog menu topics. Whenever you add a new course to the system, you associate it with one or more menu topics that determine where it can be found in the course catalog.

Course Details Page

When people search or browse the catalog, they eventually see a list of courses. Selecting a course from the list takes them to a course details page that lists all the course properties and provides a way to enroll in the course. When you add a new course to the system, you populate all the properties that will appear on the course details page, such as title, description, and credits.

Metadata

A course details page may list other information beyond the course title, description, and credits. For example, there may be a fee charged for the course. In many LMS products, you can configure a set of descriptive properties that course owners can use to "tag" their course. These properties are often referred to as metadata, which are essentially data that describe other data.

In an LMS, you can use metadata properties to describe the course delivery mode, the product line or business unit with which the course is associated, or any other descriptive information useful to your organization.

Configurable Course Structures

A course may involve a scheduled event, a self-paced module, assignments, tests, surveys, or other types of learning activities. Many LMS products provide a way to configure course structures that allow you to set up any number of these activities in any combination.

You can configure the course structure so that the activities must be taken sequentially, can be taken in any order, or a mix of the two. For example, your course could require a pretest that must be completed before any other activity, followed by a set of assignments and self-paced work that can be completed in any order, and ending with a post-test and course completion survey.

You can configure the course structure so that people must complete all activities, a minimum number of activities, or a subset of required activities to get credit for completing the course.

Every LMS product takes a slightly different approach to supporting the configuration of these course structures. If you are thinking about getting a new LMS, it is a good idea to make a list of the types of course structures you will need to support and make sure they are supported by the product you are considering.

Learning Event Scheduling

If your organization offers training events, either in a physical classroom or virtually, your LMS will need to support learning event scheduling. To configure a learning event in your LMS, you will need to create a course in the catalog first and then schedule offerings of the course, or classes. Each class will have a start date and time, end date and time, instructor, and location.

LMS products differ in how they support scheduled learning events. If you need to handle complex scheduling, such as a class that is held in one location on Monday from 9 to 11:30 a.m.

with one instructor, at another location on Wednesday from 1 to 4 p.m. with a different instructor, and back to the first location on Friday from 1 to 3 p.m. with the original instructor, then your LMS will need to support courses with class offerings that occur in multiple sessions.

Some LMS products support self-paced online courses and do not support events at all. There are other products that support events, but do not support the concept of multiple sessions. Some cannot handle multiple instructors working as a tag team to teach a course. It is important that you make sure your LMS supports the way you need to manage your learning event scheduling.

Resource Management

Any LMS that supports learning event scheduling must also provide a way to configure a list of instructors and a list of training locations. When you schedule a learning event, you associate it with the location in which it will occur and one or more instructors who will teach it.

In many LMS products, locations are made up of a hierarchical list of buildings and rooms within each building. The LMS lists the building address and room number in the event description and includes this information in the confirmation email message sent to people when they enroll in the event.

LMS products often allow you to set up each instructor with an optional photo, bio, professional credentials, and other information that may be displayed in the event description. Some LMS products automatically detect and flag conflicts, such as double scheduling of an instructor or location.

In addition to instructors and locations, some LMS products support an equipment list. Equipment may include easels, flipcharts, markers, whiteboards, computers, Internet connectivity, or items needed for hands-on training. You can configure the equipment that your organization uses and associate the appropriate equipment with a scheduled learning event.

Publishing Workflow

Your course is not generally available in the LMS until it is "published," which makes it visible and accessible to end users. This means that you can create a course and configure its properties without people seeing it. Then, when you are ready for people to take the new course, you publish it. LMS course publishing is a process that usually involves several steps that can be thought of as a workflow.

The publishing workflow in some LMS products is predefined and cannot be changed. In other products, it has configurable parameters that enable organizations to establish an approval process. When approval is required, a course owner who is ready to publish actually submits the course for publication. One or more approvers are automatically notified and can review the course to ensure it meets the organization's publishing criteria and then approve or reject it. Some LMS products provide a way for the reviewer to give a reason for rejection and notes on what the course owner should do to resubmit the course. A few LMS products support multiple levels of approval.

Course Equivalencies

Some LMS products support course equivalencies—a set of two or more courses, any of which can be taken to meet a curriculum or regulatory compliance requirement. To use this feature, you establish a curriculum or compliance goal and select all the courses required to achieve the goal, some of which might include course equivalencies. For example, to achieve a first aid certification, you can complete a course from the American Red Cross or an equivalent course from another approved provider.

Course Prerequisites

Some LMS products support course prerequisites. You can use prerequisites to ensure people who take your course are already prepared with the appropriate baseline skills and knowledge. For example, you may require people to complete a fundamentals course before they are allowed to register for an advanced course. When a prerequisite relationship is established between two courses, the prerequisite course is usually listed, automatically, on the course details page of the course for which it is a prerequisite.

Some LMS products enable you to configure a prerequisite as recommended or enforced. A recommended prerequisite does not preclude your users from registering for the course for which it is a prerequisite, while an enforced prerequisite will not allow them to register without first completing the prerequisite course. Some LMS products support more than one prerequisite for a single course.

Curricula

A curriculum is a collection of courses. People who register for the curriculum must complete all course requirements to get credit. This is another feature that is not supported by all LMS products and, when it is supported, may be implemented with varying amounts of power and flexibility.

Curriculum administration can have complex requirements. For example, you may need to establish a sequence in which courses may be taken and identify which are required, optional, and equivalent. You may or may not want people who enroll in the curriculum to be automatically enrolled in its courses. If your curriculum contains courses A, B, and C, and a person has already completed course B before enrolling in the curriculum, you may or may not want that course completion to count toward curriculum completion. If you require curriculum support, make sure your LMS curriculum features fully support your needs.

Web-Based Course Hosting, Running, and Version Control

Web-based course hosting refers to an LMS's ability to store course content files and directories. This is convenient for some organizations, while others may choose to host their course files on one or more separate servers, called remote content servers.

Regardless of where the course files are stored, the LMS must be able to launch, track, and report on self-paced online courses. This LMS capability is most reliable with courses that are based on standards such as SCORM, AICC, xAPI, and cmi5. Many LMS products support SCORM and AICC. As demand grows for newer specifications—xAPI and cmi5—more LMS products are supporting those as well. These standards and others are discussed in more detail in chapter 5.

You may want to make changes to an online course and create a new version. If so, you will need to use your LMS's version control features. At a minimum, version control enables you to publish a new version of the same course, giving it a different version number but retaining the rest of the course properties and its place in the course catalog. Ideally, your LMS will enable you to run reports on everyone who has taken any version of the course, or people who have taken a specific version.

Because standards-based online courses are often self-paced, it can be challenging to publish a new version without interrupting people who are taking the course and whose data are associated with the previous version. To address this, many LMS products provide options for you to:

- Allow people who are actively taking the previous version to continue and complete that version while all new enrollments go to the new version.
- Require anyone who is active in the course to start over in the new version.
- Require people who have completed an older version of the course to retake the new version.

The first of these options is often preferred, but the other two options can be very useful when delivering compliance training, or when making important changes to the course.

Coursework Assignments

Some LMS products provide a way for a course instructor to create an assignment by posting instructions and optionally uploading materials that can be downloaded by learners. Learners can follow the instructions and either click a box to attest to the fact that they completed the assignment or upload assignment documents. The instructor can review any work uploaded by learners and take an LMS action to confirm that they have completed the assignment.

Survey Creation and Administration

While many organizations use third-party online survey tools, some LMS products have built-in tools for creating, administering, and reporting on surveys. LMS survey tools usually support several question types, such as multiple choice (select one, select all that apply); Likert scale; short answer; and free response. Surveys differ from tests in that they are not scored. You can view reports of individual or aggregated survey results.

Many organizations distribute surveys to learners upon course completion to gauge their reactions to the course. Some organizations distribute surveys to the learner's manager several weeks or months after course completion to collect opinions and observations on whether the learner's behavior or job performance changed as a result of applying what was covered in the course. If you plan to use your LMS survey tools with these goals in mind, make sure your LMS can support standard survey questions that can be reported across multiple courses, all versions of an online course, all offerings of an instructor-led course, and all classes taught by a specific instructor.

Test Creation and Administration

Sometimes, tests are built into online courses with the results reported through an LMS. Some organizations create and administer tests and report results using a third-party, dedicated testing platform, which may or may not be integrated with the LMS. Many LMS products also provide built-in test features.

LMS products that offer testing features usually offer a variety of question types, which may include some combination of multiple choice (select one, select all that apply); Boolean (true/false, yes/no); short answer; matching; and more. Some products support advanced features like question pools, where a test can randomly present questions from the pool, and other features like random question order, question weighting, question groups, and timed questions. You can set a cut score. People who achieve the cut score or higher pass the test. Some products enable you to configure the maximum number of times a learner can retake the test and whether to count the most recent score or the highest score achieved across multiple attempts.

You can run reports on individual and aggregate test results. Some systems provide item analysis reports to help you check the quality of your questions. For example, if a large percentage of people answer the same question with the same wrong answer, you may determine that the question is written ambiguously, or the answer options are not distinct enough for people to discriminate between them. This information can help you improve the validity and reliability of your test.

Credits

LMS products typically allow you to configure any number of credit types, such as clock hours, continuing education units, or continuing professional education credits. You can associate a course with a specific number of credits for one or more credit types so that people who complete the course are awarded the credits.

Completion Certificates

Like many companies, your organization may need to provide a personalized, nicely formatted course completion certificate that can be viewed, saved, and printed by people who complete a course. Your certificate may need to include the name of the course, the name of the person who completed it, the completion date, credits awarded, and other information.

LMS products usually allow you to create any number of course completion certificate templates. Some organizations use multiple templates to represent different business units or curricula, or to differentiate between employee and customer training. Template setup is done by an authorized administrator who specifies the layout, imports any graphics, defines fonts and sizes, and enters nonvariable text and placeholders for variables such as learner name, course name, completion date, and credits awarded.

User-Course Interactions

We've already established that an LMS has users and courses. Users interact with courses in a corporate LMS by doing things like enrolling, getting on a waiting list, expressing interest, earning a certification or recertification, accessing online courses, or viewing a personalized transcript.

Self-Enrollment

A key benefit of an LMS is its ability to support self-service. People can search or browse the course catalog, find a relevant course, and self-enroll. After enrolling for an online course, they get immediate access to the course. After enrolling in an event-based course, people can select the date and location of the offering that best fits their schedule to reserve a seat in the class. All of this can be done without any delays or need for the involvement of an administrator, registrar, or instructor.

Enrollment Approval

There may be times when you want to configure a course so that enrollments must be approved by a manager or administrator before they are finalized. Some LMS products enable people to request enrollment in a course. The system notifies one or more designated approvers who can review the request and approve or deny it. This feature may be useful to organizations that need to manage training budgets carefully or ensure that only qualified people gain access to a course.

Enrollment by an Instructor or Administrator

If you ever need to set up a private class for people at their work location, you may want to have an administrator or instructor register the people in the class. Most LMS products provide a way for an administrator or instructor to enroll one or more people in a class.

Automatic Enrollment

Some organizations provide training that is mandatory for a group of employees. In this case, you may want to automatically enroll everyone who belongs to a user group in a mandatory course. For example, your company employs forklift operators who must complete a course to meet OSHA compliance.

Maximum Class Size and Wait List

A wait list is a feature that automates the management of overbooked classes. If your organization offers instructor-led training, you may need to define a maximum class size. After the number of people enrolling in the class reaches the maximum class size, any additional enrollees can be presented with the option to be placed on a wait list.

You can monitor the wait list. If it becomes very long, you might decide to move the class to a location with greater capacity and increase the maximum class size, or schedule additional class offerings to meet the demand.

If someone withdraws from the class, people on the wait list are automatically notified and given the option to join the class. Some LMS products notify everyone on the list and the seat goes to the first person who responds. Some products will notify the first wait-listed person and give them time to respond. If that person has not taken the seat or responded within the given timeframe, the next person is notified, and this process continues until the seat is taken. Although notifying wait-listed people sequentially is perhaps the fairest approach, a late cancellation that requires a quick response may necessitate notifying all wait-listed people simultaneously. Some products provide both options, allowing you to decide which method to use on a course-by-course basis.

Express Interest

An unfortunate situation that I have seen happen many times is where people spend valuable time and effort searching and browsing the LMS catalog, find the exact course they want to take, and then cannot register because there is either nothing scheduled close by, nothing at a time fitting their schedule, or worse yet, no offerings scheduled at all. This can be very frustrating to LMS users. Some LMS products provide a way for people who find themselves in this situation to click a button that indicates they are interested in taking the course. Clicking this button adds that person to a list of people who have expressed interest in the course.

You can monitor this feature and respond by scheduling new offerings of the course in the appropriate locations. People on the list are automatically notified when a new offering has been scheduled and, upon enrolling, are automatically removed from the express interest list. This is a very useful feature; however, relatively few LMS vendors offer it.

Certification and Recertification

Many organizations are concerned with meeting regulatory compliance requirements, which often require proof that employees have received training. Compliance may also require that the training be refreshed periodically, such as every year or every two years. Many LMS products handle this need through a set of features called certification and recertification.

You can associate a course with compliance certification and configure it to expire in some number of months, after which time recertification is required. You can then assign the course to specific employees or those in a specified user group who need to meet the certification requirement. If needed, you can set a due date by which time employees must complete the initial certification training. Any employee who has not completed the training successfully by the due date is notified, with a copy to their manager. Once an employee completes the training, the LMS initiates an automatic countdown toward expiration. A few weeks before the expiration date is reached, the employee is automatically notified that it is time to get recertified and reassigned to the training course.

Active Course List

After enrolling, people must be able to view a personalized list of their active courses—that is, the courses they are enrolled in and have not yet completed. An LMS will provide a place where people can view these courses and launch web-based training, tests, surveys, and other online learning modules.

Transcript

An LMS transcript provides a personalized list of all courses a user has completed, the credits they have earned for each, and a way to view or print a course completion certificate.

Email Notifications

Anyone who has shopped online has received email notifications that confirm the purchase, indicate the product has shipped, and announce its delivery. In the same way, an LMS provides notifications to confirm transactions, or alert or remind users of actions to take.

Most LMS products provide an array of notifications out of the box. You can disable, enable, and customize each of these notifications. You can modify the message recipients as well as the message subject and body. You can plug in dynamic data fields that represent the username, course name, dates, and other system-generated information.

Email notifications are important, but if overused may be ignored by users. It is important to enable only the most useful notifications and disable the rest.

Administration Features

To properly manage learning, LMS administrators need to be able to perform certain tasks. These tasks include configuring the course catalog, creating and publishing courses, taking attendance, running reports, and much more.

Administrator Roles, Permissions, and Span of Control

Most LMS products allow you to define and configure your own administrator roles, sometimes referred to as security roles, and set permissions for what each role is allowed to do in the system. Permissions allow you to grant or restrict access to specific LMS features and content at a granular level. You can then assign people to each administrator role.

An administrator's span of control is related to where, in the organization hierarchy, they have been assigned permissions. You can assign a person to an administrator role for a specific organization and all the organizations under it in the hierarchy. So, for example, one person may have permission to publish courses and run reports for the entire company, while another may be able to do so for the sales division only. This approach lets an organization configure the LMS to support learning program administration in a way that reflects how the organization operates.

Batch Enrollments

In some cases, an LMS administrator or instructor may need to enroll multiple users in a class. Rather than selecting users and enrolling them one at a time, an LMS may provide a batch method that allows you to identify a group of users through profile information, work location, organization, or job information and enroll them all at once. Some LMS products allow a list of enrollees to be imported from a spreadsheet for batch enrollment in a course.

Class Rosters

An instructor may need access to a roster of all people who have enrolled in a class. The instructor can use this roster to take attendance and change enrollee status in the course to *attended, completed, no-show,* and so on.

Gradebook

When a course involves multiple activities such as events, self-paced modules, assignments, tests, and surveys, you may want to keep track of people's progress. You can do this with an LMS gradebook. The gradebook displays the user's status and test scores for a multiactivity course or curriculum.

Proctored and Timed Tests

A few LMS products provide the capability for you to administer a proctored or timed test. Proctored tests are administered with an authorized observer in the room, who opens and closes access to the test. Timed tests provide an automated timer that opens and closes access to the test within a configurable timeframe.

Reporting Features

One of the key benefits of an LMS is its ability to track learning data and produce reports. Organizations use LMS reports to determine who is using their learning programs, which programs are most popular, the number of credits people have earned, and much more. Reporting is especially important to organizations that need proof that they are meeting training requirements for regulatory compliance or to dispute claims that an employee who was dismissed due to poor performance may not have received necessary training.

It is important to note that only a subset of LMS data is available in reports. Many times, custom-defined user profile fields and course metadata values are not available for use in report result sets or filtering selections. Identify your most critical reporting needs and work with your LMS vendor to make sure you can get those reports from the system.

You might be tempted to want reports on lots of data, viewable in lots of different ways. For every report, you should consider who needs the data, how often, and for what purpose. Too often, I have seen organizations create dozens or even hundreds of reports and then end up using only a handful of them. Before requesting a custom report, it is important that you define who, specifically, needs the report, how often it will be used, and what decisions can be made or actions taken as a result of the report data.

Typically, LMS products provide a set of canned reports that can be customized with filtering and sorting options. Many LMS products allow you to export reports to a variety of formats, such as HTML, PDF, or Excel. Some allow you to schedule reports to be run and emailed to a list of recipients automatically. Others offer more sophisticated reporting features, such as dashboards and analytics.

Canned Reports

Most LMS products provide a wide selection of the types of canned reports that are most commonly needed, such as all people who have enrolled in or completed a specific learning activity or set of learning activities, and all learning activities that a specific person or set of people has enrolled in or completed.

You can apply filters to these and other reports to produce a more specific data set. Report filters include items you can select or enter, like those listed in Table 2-1.

Table 2-1. Examples of Report Filters

Report Filter	Example
A Date Range	• Start of the fiscal year to the current date • Start and end dates representing the previous quarter
A Specific Course or Course Group	• All courses in a curriculum • All health and safety courses • All regulatory compliance courses
A Specific User or User Group	• All users in a plant or office location • All employees hired in the last six weeks • All outbound call center sales agents

Report Filter	Example
User Status	Users whose status is or was: • enrolled • dropped • in progress • not completed • completed and failed • completed and passed.

Because an LMS contains a roster of people enrolled in a class, many LMS products provide special reports that enable instructors to print sign-in sheets to help with attendance tracking and tent cards or name tags for attendees. Of course, tent cards and name tags require heavier card stock or specially designed paper for your printer.

Custom Reports

Many LMS products provide a way to generate custom reports. Sometimes, a web-based form is provided where various data fields and filtering and sorting options can be selected. Once an administrator completes and submits the custom report form, the LMS queries its database using the selected values and generates a report. Table 2-2 describes some examples of the types of parameters you might set to create a custom LMS report.

Table 2-2. Examples of Custom Report Parameters

Custom Report Parameters	Example
The data fields you select determine what shows up in the report.	Selecting the fields *course name, course code,* and *course published date* will produce a report containing three columns, with each row representing a course that lists the data in those three fields.
Filters limit the result set.	Entering a date range filter eliminates all data that fall outside the selected start and end dates.
Sorting determines which data field will be used to set the data order.	Sorting on course name will order the result set by course name.

Some LMS products provide integrations with popular third-party reporting tools. Many LMS vendors offer fee-based custom report creation services to customers.

Export Reports to Various Formats

The default format for most LMS reports is hypertext markup language, or HTML, which you can view in your web browser. Most LMS products allow you to export a report to other formats as well. Table 2-3 lists the types of report formats you might find in an LMS and describes the advantage of each format. Keep in mind that each LMS product will support its own subset of these report formats.

Table 2-3. Examples of Report Formats

Format	Advantages
Hypertext Markup Language (HTML)	A format that you can view in your browser.
Portable Document Format (PDF)	A good format for reports that you need to print or email to people.
Microsoft Excel (XLS or XLSX)	A format that allows you to manipulate the data by sorting, filtering, or reformatting them.
Comma Separated Values (CSV)	A file format that you can open and use in Excel. It's particularly useful if your LMS cannot export directly to Excel.
eXtensible Markup Language (XML)	A format that is useful for exporting LMS data so that they can be imported into another system.

Automated Report Scheduling and Distribution

Many LMS products allow you to establish a recurring schedule, such as monthly or quarterly, for a specific report to be generated automatically. You can also create an email distribution list for the report. Whenever the report is scheduled to run, it is automatically emailed to everyone on the distribution list.

Some LMS products require that everyone on the distribution list has an LMS account and permission to view the report. In these systems, you create the distribution list by selecting a group of user IDs. The email people on the distribution list receive contains a link to the report. Message recipients can click the link to access the LMS and view the report in their web browser.

Other products allow you to distribute reports to people who are not LMS users. In these systems, you create the distribution list by entering a list of email addresses. The email people on the list receive contains the report as a file attachment, often in PDF format.

Dashboards and Analytics

Many LMS products can generate graphical reports that represent high-level data in pie charts, bar charts, cluster charts, heat maps, and other formats. Often, you can click on the graphic to drill down to more detailed data in text-based reports. Some LMS products provide "widgets" representing graphical reports. You can select any of the widgets to create a custom dashboard.

Other Feature Options

Now that we've discussed the essential features of a corporate LMS, let's move on to some special features. LMS vendors sometimes add these special features to differentiate their product from their competitors'. These features may support things like social networking, e-commerce, and competency management. Some vendors offer complementary products, such as talent management suites that are fully integrated with the LMS.

Messaging and Discussion Boards

Some LMS products include features for communication and social networking. Messaging allows LMS users to communicate with one another in a way that is similar to email. Discussion boards provide a way for people to create topics and post or reply to questions and comments. If you are interested in these types of features, ask your vendor whether messaging and discussion board features are available and, if so, whether they are limited to cohorts in the same course or class or whether they are open to all LMS users.

I have found that most corporate organizations tend to use, rather than their LMS, other business platforms that have a more specialized focus on social networking and collaboration. However, messaging can be useful for announcements related to the LMS system, and discussion boards can be a useful ingredient in blended learning programs.

Ask This

Ask your vendor whether messaging and discussion board features are available and, if so, whether they are limited to cohorts in the same course or class or open to all LMS users.

Manager View

Some LMS products can track the reporting relationships between people and their managers. This is often done by adding a manager's LMS user ID to each user's profile. These reporting relationships can be used to provide managers a view into the learning activities and achievements of their direct reports.

Some systems enable managers to assign training to their direct reports. These features are helpful to organizations in which managers are actively involved in the learning and development of people who report to them.

Extended Enterprise

While many organizations use an LMS for employee training, some are also concerned with training customers and partners, such as suppliers, dealers, and distributors. This model is often referred to as the extended enterprise.

Organizations that deliver training to the extended enterprise must have tight control over what content each user group can see and access. LMS products that support this model typically enable you to create different sites, or domains, in the LMS. This allows each group to have its own URL to access the LMS, its own homepage, its own content, and its own course catalog. Each site may have a different set of administrators and produce a different set of reports. You can configure the features and workflows differently for each site. For example, you can enable e-commerce features for customers and disable them for employees. You can restrict proprietary courses to be viewable by employees only and make other courses available to all groups.

E-Commerce

If your organization needs to charge users for courses, you will need an LMS product that supports e-commerce. These products typically provide a shopping cart and checkout experience. Payment for courses may be processed using a credit card, purchase order, or other method.

Some LMS products provide a way for a customer to purchase a credit that can be debited when anyone in the customer organization enrolls in a fee-based course. If your organization accepts payments using a credit card or PayPal, you will need to contract with a third-party payment processing vendor. Find out which payment processing vendors are supported by your LMS. While you can often choose from a list of supported vendors, many products support the configuration of only one payment processing vendor at a time.

Some organizations need to handle interdepartmental billing in their LMS. While this is not the same as e-commerce, it is an accounting process to manage course funding. If you need to handle this type of accounting in your LMS, you will need to find a product that can associate a course with a sponsoring organization, the organization that purchased the course. Every time someone enrolls for the course, the enrollee's organization is charged a fee, which is paid to the sponsoring organization. This may be handled manually using LMS reports, or it may be automated through integration between the LMS and the organization's general ledger. More information on LMS integration with a general ledger can be found in chapter 8.

Competency Management

Some organizations use competency models to describe job requirements. A competency is an observable behavior that can be described at various levels of proficiency. A novice may not know what needs to be done, let alone how to go about doing it. A less experienced practitioner may have baseline competence, like an understanding of what needs to be done, but limited ability to do it well. A more experienced practitioner may have advanced competence—that is, the ability to do it pretty well, fairly consistently. An expert may excel, being able to do it extremely well all the time.

Each job role may have its own set of competencies, each at a required proficiency level. Together, these competencies and proficiency levels define a standard for effective performance in the job role. So, to be effective in that role, a person must be able to demonstrate competence at the required proficiency level.

Some LMS products support competency models, allowing administrators to enter them or import them from another system spreadsheet. Once entered into the LMS, competencies can be associated with jobs, people, and courses.

Some LMS products automatically generate a job-specific, competency-based self-assessment. People can use these self-assessments to improve in their current job role or prepare for a new one. If an employee wants to improve in their current role, the system knows their job, based on their user profile, and presents them with a self-assessment where they can rate their proficiency level for each competency their job requires. Their self-ratings are then compared with the job standards, and they can view the competencies where they exceed, meet, or do not meet the job standard. For any areas where they do not meet the standard, training may be recommended. If they want to prepare for a new role, the system provides a way for them to select their desired role and compare their self-assessed competencies with the standards for that role. They can use the results to create a professional development plan.

Three general cautions about competencies:

1. A lot of rigor is required to use competencies effectively, because inconsistencies in position titles and job descriptions can make it difficult to define job roles and standards. To be used effectively, competencies must be written at a consistent level of detail across all job roles.
2. While a proficiency scale may be applied consistently to all competencies, the challenge will be to describe what each level of proficiency looks like, when observed, for each competency, in the context of each job role.
3. Courses are typically focused on learning objectives rather than competencies and proficiency levels. It can be difficult to map a course with the appropriate competencies and proficiency level if it was not purposefully designed and developed to focus on those competencies.

Key Takeaways

This chapter described the features that are available with corporate LMS products:

- A corporate LMS is used to deliver learning programs to employees and, in some cases, to customers and business partners.
- A snapshot of corporate LMS features is shown in Table 2-4.

Table 2-4. Snapshot of Corporate LMS Features

User Management	• User accounts • Authentication • User profiles • Job roles and organizations • User groups or audiences • Role-based views
Course Management	• Course catalog • Metadata • Configurable course structures • Learning event scheduling • Resource management • Publishing workflow • Course equivalencies and prerequisites • Curricula • Web-based courses • Surveys and tests • Credits • Completion certificates
User-Course Interactions	• Enrollment methods • Maximum class sizes and wait lists • A way to express interest in a course • Certification and recertification • Personalized access to active courses • Transcripts • Email notifications
Administration	• Administrator permissions • Batch enrollments • Class rosters • Gradebooks • Proctored and timed tests

Table 2-4. Snapshot of Corporate LMS Features (cont.)

Reporting	• Canned reports • Sign-in sheets • Tent cards • Name badges • Custom reports • Options for automatic scheduling and distribution of reports • Dashboards and analytics
Others	• Messaging • Discussion boards • Manager view of employee training • Support for extended enterprise • E-commerce • Competency management

The next chapter introduces the features that are available in another type of product: the academic LMS.

CHAPTER 3

Academic LMS Features

This chapter describes what an academic LMS is and how it differs from a corporate LMS. It covers the features of an academic LMS that allow you to manage users and courses and administer the system.

An academic LMS is very different from a corporate LMS. An academic LMS is a system for developing, managing, and delivering learning content in the context of an online classroom that replaces or augments a physical classroom. While one or more super-administrators manage the LMS technology and grant instructor permissions to faculty, the primary administrators of an academic LMS are instructors, professors, and teachers.

Academic LMS products are used in a variety of settings, including primary, secondary, and higher education; continuous adult education; government; professional associations; and business settings. In an academic setting, courses often span a semester, during which an instructor works with a class of student cohorts through various materials, activities, assignments, and tests. In other settings, courses are more likely to be shorter but still emphasize the instructor and cohort model.

Let's say you work at a college or university. Your institution offers continuing education programs on evenings and weekends. While your programs have many students who live close by and can attend classes on campus, you want to expand beyond your campus to offer online classes that can be attended by anyone, from anywhere. You can use an academic LMS to deliver virtual classes online. As an instructor, you can interact with students as a group or one-on-one, and students can interact with one another. You can post course materials and assignments, administer quizzes and tests, and track student progress.

As with a corporate LMS, these systems offer features for user management, course management, and administration. The key differences lie in how these features are designed by the vendors and used by customers.

User Management Features

The user management features of an academic LMS include user account creation, authentication, user profiles, and roles and permissions. While all these features are also present in a corporate LMS, they are often managed differently in an academic LMS, especially in academic environments. Table 3-1 lists the key similarities and differences between the user management features of a corporate and academic LMS.

Course Management Features

Managing courses in an academic LMS is very different from doing so in a corporate LMS. An academic LMS is focused on the way courses are taught in academic environments and includes features to:

- Manage lessons and assignments.
- Post a course syllabus, learning goals, and schedule.
- Provide interactive activities such as surveys, quizzes, and polls.
- Upload and download multimedia course materials.
- Conduct web conferences.
- Send instructor-student messages and messages among students.
- Send multimedia feedback—that is, audio, video, and text—from the instructor to each student.
- Post and reply to multimedia discussion topics.
- Establish student groups and collaborative workspaces for breakout sessions and class projects.

Table 3-1. Comparing Corporate and Academic LMS User Management Features

Feature	Similarities	Differences
User Accounts	• Both contain user accounts made up of a unique user ID, username, and password. • When implemented in a corporate setting, both may import user accounts from a human resource management system.	Academic LMS: When implemented in an academic setting, user accounts are usually created manually by an instructor or administrator.
Authentication	• Users log in with a username and password and are authenticated—that is, matched with the appropriate user account, and authorized to use the system. • When implemented in a corporate setting, both often use single sign-on to allow users to access multiple corporate systems with a single login.	Academic LMS: When implemented in an academic setting, single sign-on is usually not needed.
User Profile	• The user profile in both is a collection of data that describe the user.	Academic LMS: The user profile also includes a personal online portfolio of the student's course materials and coursework.
Permissions	• Permissions to administer system features can be assigned at a granular level.	Academic LMS: Instructors have full permissions to manage the classes they teach and can assign specific permissions to students.

Lessons and Assignments

As an instructor, you can create lessons for a class. Lessons can include presentations, assignments, quizzes, and other materials and activities. You can create lessons from scratch or import a copy of a lesson or assignment from another class and then modify it. You can post instructions and a due date for any number of assignments, along with materials students need to complete each assignment. You can configure the system to send email reminders to students automatically when assignment due dates are approaching or past due. You can also view and grade the work students turn in.

Students can view assignment instructions and download the materials. After completing an assignment, students can turn in their work by uploading documents to the system.

Syllabus, Learning Goals, and Schedule

You can publish a course syllabus, the learning objectives or goals for the course, and a course schedule. Students can view this information before registering and any time after registering for the course. The course schedule is particularly useful to set students' expectations and allocate sufficient time for assignments, study, and other coursework.

Surveys, Quizzes, and Polls

You can create a quiz or survey in the system. The LMS provides a variety of question types that may include multiple choice (select one, select all that apply); Boolean (true/false, yes/no); matching; Likert scale; short answer; and essay. Some products support question pools, random question ordering, question weights, and question groups. Tests can be configured for automatic or manual scoring; the latter is usually required for tests that include essay questions.

You can post polling questions for the class at any time. After students respond to the poll, you can view the results and have the option to share them with the students.

You can share your surveys, quizzes, and polls with other instructors, who can then make a copy and reuse or modify them for use in another class. You can run reports to view survey, quiz, and poll results for a specific course or all the courses where it is used. Item analysis reports enable you to check the reliability and validity of your quizzes and surveys.

Multimedia Course Materials

Some academic LMS products provide a way for you to manage your own searchable repository of course materials. The repository may be organized into files and folders and can include instructional materials in a wide variety of formats, such as text, images, audio, and video. You can tag your materials with descriptive information and have the option to share specific materials with other instructors.

Web Conferencing

While corporate LMS products may provide out-of-the-box integration with a third-party web-conferencing platform, many academic LMS products have built-in web-conferencing capabilities. Web conferencing allows an instructor and the students to access a common URL, sign in, and participate in an online group session. As an instructor, you can share your screen with students or allow a student to share their screen with the rest of the class. Typically, mouse and keyboard control resides with the person whose screen is being shared, but you have the option to establish remote control of another person's screen. Audio communication for the web conference can occur over the phone, the Internet, or both.

In addition to screen sharing, web conferences include features for private and public chats, polling questions, posting web links, and more. You can view icons that indicate who is speaking, who has a hand raised, or who likes, doesn't like, or is confused about what is being presented. Some systems also provide a cue indicating whether the web-conferencing window is behind other windows on a student's desktop, which may mean that the student is not paying attention.

Many systems allow you to record the entire web conference, including what is viewed and what is said. The instructor can make the recordings available as a video for later access by students who may have missed the session, or for later review by the class.

Instant Messaging

Instant messaging features enable you, the instructor, to communicate online with students, or students to communicate with one another. You can message a single student, a group of students, or the entire class. Classmates can message one another individually or in groups. These communications can be valuable in Q&A sessions, group study, and collaborative projects.

Multimedia Feedback

You, the instructor, can provide feedback to students in a variety of ways using different media. Many academic LMS products enable instructors to use any combination of text, audio, and video to communicate their feedback. Some products provide optional video capture and editing equipment and tools, making it easy to use video in course materials, messaging, and feedback to students.

Discussion Boards

Some academic LMS products offer discussion boards where you and your students can create topics, post and reply to one another, like one another's posts and replies, and follow a discussion or another user. You can configure a discussion board to be accessible to all participants in a single class or to a broader set of students who are actively using the LMS.

Student Groups and Collaborative Workspaces

Some LMS products enable you to create student groups for class projects and breakout sessions. You can establish collaborative workspaces, or virtual breakout rooms, where each student group "meets" to share materials, message one another, give one another feedback, post and reply to discussions, and conduct web conferences.

Administration Features

In any type of LMS, administration features are those that require special permission and, generally, are not accessible to students. In an academic LMS, you may have one or a small group of super-administrators who manage the LMS technology and assign permissions to instructors, but the primary, and most active, administrators of an academic LMS are instructors, professors, and teachers.

Academic LMS administration features include class rosters and gradebooks, reports, analytics and statistics, and tools for developing courses and lessons in the system.

Online Classroom

You can create any number of online classrooms for the classes you offer. Each online classroom contains your lessons, materials, and other resources for the class.

Roster and Gradebook

A student roster is a list of all the people in your class. When students log in to the system, they are able to access a list of online classes in which they're enrolled. As the instructor, you can use a gradebook to track attendance, assignment completion, quiz scores, and other information for each student in the roster.

Reports, Analytics, and Statistics

Academic LMS products provide reports on areas that help you manage your classes, such as:

- the last time each of your students accessed your online classroom
- how much time each student spent in the online classroom
- each student's status for an assignment, such as on time or late, and graded or ungraded
- each student's progress in the course
- each student's access to your course materials
- quiz and survey results and statistics
- a listing of all the courses and course materials you've created in the system.

Key Takeaways

This chapter described the features that are available in academic LMS products and how they differ from those of a corporate LMS. The key takeaways are:

- An academic LMS is used as a virtual classroom environment to replace or augment a physical classroom.
- Academic LMS products are used in a wide variety of settings, including higher education, continuous adult education, government, and professional associations. Businesses sometimes use an academic LMS in combination with a corporate LMS.
- A snapshot of academic LMS features is shown in Table 3-2.

Table 3-2. Snapshot of Academic LMS Features

User Management	• User accounts • Authentication • User profiles • Permissions
Course Management	• Lessons and assignments • Course syllabus and schedule • Surveys, quizzes, and polls • Multimedia course materials • Web conferences • Messaging students • Messages among students • Discussion topics • Breakout sessions
Administration	• Permissions management • Online classroom creation • Class roster and gradebook • Reports, analytics, and statistics
Reporting	• Canned reports • Student visits, time spent, and activity in the virtual class • Student assignment status and progress in the course • Survey and test results • Learning materials listings

The next chapter explores the features of the third type of LMS product: an LCMS-LMS.

CHAPTER 4

LCMS-LMS Features

This chapter describes what an LCMS-LMS is and how it compares with a corporate LMS. It also describes the features of an LCMS-LMS that allow you to manage users and course content, and develop and deliver courses.

An integrated LCMS-LMS is similar to a corporate LMS, but it has added capabilities for developing and managing learning content. Several LCMS products offer robust content development capabilities, but have none of the course delivery features found in an LMS. However, there are a growing number of LCMS-LMS products that allow you to develop courses and course materials in the same system that delivers the courses to end users.

An LCMS-LMS is targeted, primarily, at organizations that develop their own instructional programs. These products are frequently used by businesses that design and deliver their own employee training, professional organizations that develop and deliver courses to their members, or organizations whose business is selling courses to customers. They are typically not used by organizations that do mostly instructor-led training or those that develop courses using popular authoring tools, hire vendors to develop online courses using their own tools, or use off-the-shelf courseware.

Let's say you work at a midsize business that sells products to business customers. Your products are a bit complicated, and you need to provide training to customers on how to use and maintain them. Your customers are in many time zones around the world, so instructor-led training is not an option. You can use an LCMS-LMS to deliver online, self-paced courses to your customers. Your product managers, subject matter experts, and instructional designers can collaborate to create the courses. Customers can then log in and access the training at a time of their choosing.

These systems usually offer features for user management, as well as course development and delivery.

User Management Features

The user management features of an LCMS-LMS include user account creation, authentication, user profiles, and roles and permissions. These features work in the same way as they do in corporate LMS products. The biggest difference is in the area of roles and permissions. The LCMS-related roles in an LCMS-LMS product are focused on course development, so the permissions are quite different. Table 4-1 lists the similarities and differences between the user management features of a corporate LMS and an LCMS-LMS.

Course Development Features

The course development features of an LCMS-LMS product are designed to support a team of people involved in creating courses. Some products only have simple course creation tools, while others are more advanced and may include:

- collaborative authoring tools
- a searchable content library with check-in and checkout capabilities
- content version control, global changes, and reusability
- layout templates and skins
- workflow and notifications
- content export to multiple formats.

Collaborative Authoring

Software applications that help instructional designers develop online courses are called authoring tools. There are many commercial authoring tools for individuals creating online courses. An LCMS differs from these tools in that it provides a collaborative authoring environment where a group of people can work together on developing an instructional program.

Table 4-1. Comparing Corporate and LCMS-LMS User Management Features

Feature	Similarities	Differences
User Accounts	• Both contain user accounts made up of a unique user ID, username, and password. • User accounts are usually imported from an HR management system.	LCMS-LMS: It has an additional set of users who create instructional programs.
Authentication	• Users log in with a username and password and are authenticated—that is, matched with the appropriate user account and authorized to use the system. • When implemented in a corporate setting, both often use single sign-on to allow users to access multiple corporate systems with a single login.	N/A
User Profile	• The user profile in both is a collection of data that describe the user.	N/A
Roles and Permissions	• Administrator roles are customized with specific system permissions at a granular level and assigned to people. • The roles associated with course delivery are similar to those in a corporate LMS.	LCMS-LMS: It has an additional set of development roles like course developer, graphics artist, audio and video developer, and subject matter expert.

Searchable Content Library

If you've ever developed a course and then, later, had to update it, you probably know how challenging it can be to locate and distinguish all the original source files that you had used to create graphics, icons, diagrams, videos, audio, and other course elements. An LCMS makes this process much easier by providing a searchable repository of all source and output files. Items in the repository can be tagged and described for easy discovery and retrieval. Special tools may be provided for loading, editing, storing, and retrieving audio and video content.

The library metaphor is useful, too. You can check items out to work on them and check them in when you're finished. This ensures that no one else is working on the item while you are.

Content Version Control

The LCMS-LMS library can store multiple historic versions of your content, allowing you to retrieve earlier versions so that unwanted changes can be reversed or deleted content restored.

Global Changes

Many LCMS-LMS products provide features that support global changes to content. For example, imagine the name of one of your company's products is changed. The old product name appears in multiple courses, yet you have no master index of everywhere it appears. Without an LCMS, you would need to check all the courses where you suspect the product name is referenced, identify the pages where it appears, make the changes, and republish them. Odds are you might miss a few.

With an LCMS, you simply perform a global find and replace on the product name, which is changed instantly everywhere it appears in text form. If you have followed proven practices and tagged the product name to your images, videos, or audio where the product is mentioned, those media assets are identified so that you can change them. Once all the course elements have been changed, the LCMS can provide a list of all course materials that were updated, including online courses, instructor and student guides, and job aids. This enables you to republish and redeploy all affected courses and materials.

Layout Templates and Skins

LCMS products enable you to create reusable styles so that your content has a consistent look and feel. Styles can include logos, icons, color schemes or skins, page layouts, and standardized menu and navigation controls. These templates remove duplication of effort that occurs when each course developer must create their own skins, controls, and layouts. Templates ensure a consistent look and feel for all courses and course materials, improving the user experience by making it more standardized and predictable.

Reusability

LCMS-LMS products provide several features that support content reusability. Layouts and skins can be created once and used in multiple courses and materials. Because content is stored in a centralized, searchable repository, locating existing content elements such as images, media, and even entire modules and reusing them in multiple courses becomes easy.

Workflow and Notifications

LCMS products support collaboration through a configurable set of workflow and notification options. You can schedule content development tasks, handoffs, reviews, and approvals. Your schedule triggers an automatic email alert to the person or people responsible for the next step in the content development process.

For example, an instructional designer may develop a course outline. When the outline is completed, a course author receives an email stating that it's ready. The author generates course pages from the outline. At the same time, a graphics artist is notified of images that must be created. When the graphics artist is done, the course author is notified that the images are ready to be placed into the course pages. Once the course is authored, the instructional designer is notified that the course is ready for review. After their review, the author is notified of revisions that need to be made. Next, a subject matter expert is notified that the course is ready for review.

Figure 4-1 illustrates an example of the type of learning program development workflow you can configure in an LCMS. Notice that some of the work is linear and some is done in parallel. Each handoff of work from one role to another is supported by email alerts. The entire process can be tracked by an administrator.

A dashboard shows where the course is in the development cycle, allowing a project manager to monitor its progress and intervene when delays occur. The process steps, people and roles, target dates, and sequence can be configured independently for each course development project.

Export Options

You can use the same LCMS-LMS content to generate a wide variety of course materials, including an online course, an instructor or learner guide, a job aid, documentation, or a website. This capability is especially useful for courses that you plan to offer in multiple delivery modes.

Figure 4-1. Example of Course Development Workflow

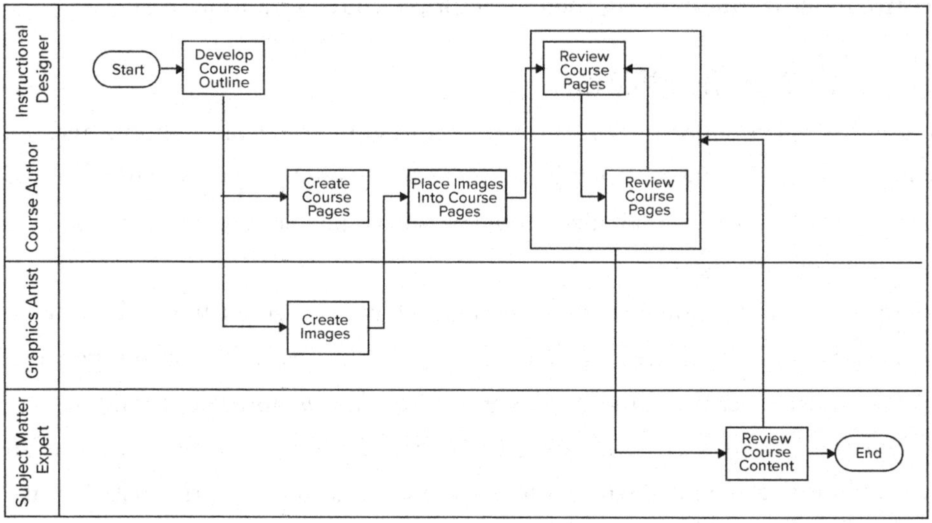

Course Delivery Features

Course delivery features generally include, at a minimum:

- a course catalog
- course self-enrollment
- web-based training delivery and tracking
- a personalized list of active courses for each user
- a personalized transcript of completed courses for each user
- email notifications
- reports.

Course Catalog

As with a corporate LMS, an LCMS-LMS supports a course catalog listing the learning programs available in the LMS. Courses may be listed by course title and code. When you select a course from the catalog, a page containing the course details is displayed, including the course description, credits, and other information, and a way to enroll in the course. You can search or browse the course catalog.

Course Self-Enrollment

LCMS-LMS products support self-service course enrollment. When you enroll in an online course, you gain immediate access to the course content. For an event-based course, you must select a specific date and location where the course is offered. It is important to note that some LCMS-LMS products are dedicated to the creation and delivery of online courses only, while other products also support event-based courses.

Web-Based Training Delivery and Tracking

LCMS-LMS products are able to host, launch, track, and report on self-paced online courses that have been developed using the product's content development capabilities. Many LCMS-LMS products do not allow you to host online courses that are developed outside of its native content development tools.

Active Courses and Transcript

After users enroll, an LCMS-LMS allows them to view a list of active courses and launch web-based training programs, tests, surveys, and other online learning modules. It also provides a transcript listing all courses they have completed, the credits earned for each course, and a way to view or print a course completion certificate.

Email Notifications

In addition to email notifications that support course development workflow, an LCMS-LMS also provides notifications related to course delivery that confirm enrollment, and alert or remind learners of actions to take.

Reports

Like a corporate LMS, LCMS-LMS products typically provide reports on items like enrollments, completions, people, and courses that can be filtered by date range, course, or user.

Key Takeaways

This chapter described the features that are available in an integrated LCMS-LMS product and how it is similar to a corporate LMS, but with added capabilities for developing and managing learning content. The key takeaways are:

- An LCMS-LMS has collaborative course development tools and some course delivery features.
- LCMS-LMS products are mostly used by organizations that develop and deliver their own learning content.
- A snapshot of integrated LCMS-LMS features is shown in Table 4-2.

Table 4-2. Snapshot of LCMS-LMS Features

User Management	• User accounts • Authentication • User profiles • Permissions
Course Development	• Collaborative authoring • A searchable content library • Content version control • Global change capabilities • Layout templates and skins • Content reusability • Workflows and notifications • Content export options
Course Delivery	• Course catalog • Course enrollment • Web-based training delivery and tracking • A personalized list of active courses and a transcript for each user • Email notifications • Reports

The next chapter introduces the various standards and specifications that are relevant to organizations that use any type of LMS.

CHAPTER 5

Relevant Technology Standards and Specifications

This chapter explains the industry standards that are relevant to an LMS. It describes the three main specifications that allow courses and the corporate LMS or LCMS-LMS to interoperate. It covers eight standards that allow the academic LMS to interoperate with other software-based teaching tools. It explains xAPI, CASS, and the total learning architecture for LMS products to interact with other technologies. It covers the WCAG and Section 508 standards for accessibility. And it describes standards for system security and data privacy.

Is your LMS accessible to people with physical or cognitive challenges? Is the system secure against hacking? Are you storing any potentially sensitive personal information about your users that must be kept private? Do you deliver self-paced e-learning courses through the LMS that must be tracked? Have you developed a lot of course and test content in your LMS that you would need to preserve if your organization were to change platforms? Do you use multiple systems to support your learning programs and need them to share a common set of data?

If you answered yes to any of these questions, you should be aware of the various technology standards and specifications relevant to learning management. There are interoperability standards for courses to work properly with an LMS and for the LMS to share data with other learning technologies; accessibility standards to enable the LMS to be used by people with visual, physical, auditory, and cognitive challenges; and standards for system security and data privacy.

LMS Interoperability Overview

There are two kinds of interoperability standards; the first is interoperability between courses and an LMS. These standards ensure that e-learning courses developed with tools outside the LMS work reliably when delivered through an LMS. The second is interoperability between learning systems. These standards allow different types of learning technologies, including the LMS, to share data.

Interoperability Between Courses and an LMS

Course-LMS interoperability standards help you publish, deliver, and track e-learning courseware in an LMS. They include AICC, SCORM, and cmi5. After you create your e-learning course, you export it to one of these standards, which provides a specification for how e-learning courses are installed on the LMS and how they communicate tracking data, such as pages visited, modules completed, and test scores, back to the LMS. Many corporate LMS and LCMS-LMS products support one or more of these standards.

Before interoperability standards existed, there was widespread frustration among organizations attempting to deliver e-learning programs. Courses purchased from different vendors required unique delivery platforms. In many situations, courses would only run on proprietary platforms provided by the course developer. If you had courseware from multiple vendors, you needed multiple platforms. Navigating multiple, disparate delivery platforms was difficult for learners and expensive for their organizations. Because courses from different vendors, who used different tools to create them, were incompatible, learning administrators couldn't combine courses into a single curriculum or compile course results into a single report or transcript. Pushback from customers, combined with advances in technology, hastened the adoption of interoperability standards.

Interoperability standards address these problems by specifying how e-learning courses need to work, or interoperate, with an LMS. Interoperability provides such compelling benefits to the marketplace that it is in the best interest of course authoring tool vendors and LMS vendors to support these standards.

There are three main facets related to courseware-LMS interoperability: course deployment, course launching, and course data tracking.

1. **Course deployment** refers to how the course is installed in the LMS. After a course is created, it is usually packaged as a data file that can be uploaded and installed on an LMS. The course may be uploaded to the LMS or a remote server. An LMS administrator creates a new course record, which has data fields for all the information the LMS needs to add the course to its catalog, such as a unique course identifier, title, and description. The course record also contains a URL to launch the course. When a course is installed on a remote server, the administrator enters the URL into the LMS. When a course is uploaded to the LMS, the URL is entered automatically.
2. **Course launching** refers to the way in which a user accesses the course through the LMS. When a user launches the course, the LMS runs the course in a "player" inside the local web browser on the user's PC, Mac, or mobile device.
3. **Course tracking** is essentially a conversation between the course and the LMS. As the user runs through the course, data are generated to track the user's progress and results. These data are located on the user's machine and must be uploaded to the LMS, which is running on a company server or in the cloud.

These three facets of courseware-LMS interoperability have been incorporated into three major interoperability standards: AICC, SCORM, and cmi5.

> A remote server is a computer on the network where web-based courses are stored and accessed by users through an LMS. The server is "remote" because it is not the LMS server. The LMS links to the web addresses of courses on the remote server.

AICC

AICC is the Aviation Industry CBT Committee standard for launching and tracking e-learning. While AICC is an older standard, some e-learning courseware is still AICC compliant, and many corporate LMS products support AICC. AICC was the first interoperability standard that enabled courses from multiple vendors to be run on a single LMS.

The AICC standard was first released in 1989 and last updated in 1998-99. The AICC specification's original purpose was to get multimedia training content developed by multiple vendors using a variety of tools to work in a standardized way on PC hardware platforms in the years prior to widespread use of Microsoft Windows. Over the years, AICC evolved with changes to tools and technologies, and, ultimately, the introduction of learning management systems in the mid-1990s. The organization behind the AICC standard disbanded in 2014 after merging its work with that of other leading standards organizations. The AICC specification is an important precursor to newer interoperability standards.

SCORM

SCORM, or Sharable Content Object Reference Model, is the Advanced Distributed Learning (ADL) standard for publishing, launching, and tracking e-learning. ADL began as a joint project of the U.S. Department of Defense and the Department of Labor, with participation from industry and other interested parties.

The SCORM standard was derived, in part, from the older AICC standard, but incorporated later developments in web technology.

ADL released the first official version of SCORM, 1.0, in January 2000. It continued to improve and expand on the specification, with subsequent releases of 1.1 in January 2001 and 1.2 in October 2001.

The next version, SCORM 2004, was released in January 2004. This version improved on the specification's support for more complex courses that contain multiple learning objectives separated into modules called shareable content objects, or SCOs. ADL released four editions of SCORM 2004. The final version was released in March 2009.

Through all its versions and improvements, SCORM has become, more or less, a turnkey solution for deploying, launching, and tracking courses through an LMS. Although earlier versions had some problems, with the later versions of SCORM, courses could be installed and run easily on any LMS that supported SCORM. This turnkey approach is very important to many course developers, who do not necessarily have advanced programming skills.

The SCORM 1.2 and SCORM 2004 specifications continue to dominate the e-learning industry. Most standards-based courses, authoring tools, and corporate LMS products support these standards. However, web technologies have continued to evolve since 2009 along with a huge increase in the use of mobile devices, which are not supported with SCORM. These factors are rapidly bringing SCORM's heyday to an end.

cmi5

Around the time the last version of SCORM was released, the standards bodies behind AICC and SCORM realized that the two standards needed to be reimagined. Both AICC and SCORM were focused on data tracking in the context of courses and could not be applied to more advanced learning and performance solutions such as performance support, knowledge management, expert networks, social media for learning, instructional games, simulations, immersive learning environments, and adaptive learning. Another key driver for the standards overhaul was the widespread use of mobile devices. The technologies underlying AICC and SCORM presented challenges to organizations that needed to track learning and performance data generated by mobile device users. These drivers led to the development of the Experience API (xAPI), which can be applied to track much more than course data and works well with mobile technologies. xAPI is much more than an interoperability standard. It provides a way to track data, not just from an LMS, but from lots of systems and applications.

Still, the need for improved courseware-LMS interoperability remained. To address this need, the AICC and ADL decided to cooperate on developing cmi5, which is an interoperability standard based on xAPI. The new specification, officially released in June 2016, is designed to do what SCORM does but in a new and improved way.

Like SCORM, cmi5 provides a turnkey approach to deploy, launch, and track online courses through an LMS. Some key advantages of cmi5 over SCORM are its ability to support mobile learning, track any type of course interaction, and eliminate the SCORM-generated pop-ups that often cause problems with pop-up blockers.

Because of these advantages, it is expected that organizations will, over time, develop cmi5 courses rather than SCORM, gradually displacing SCORM as the dominant interoperability standard between courses and the LMS.

Learning Systems Interoperability

Organizations of all types are becoming more sophisticated in their use of technology to deliver learning programs. Academic institutions are using not just an LMS, but also other educational software such as multimedia and video tools, online tutoring and assessment products, educational course materials, and digital books. Businesses, government agencies, and professional associations are using an LMS along with instructional games or simulations, knowledge management systems, performance support systems, social networking and collaboration tools, online communities, talent management systems, and workplace systems. The key question becomes, how can all these different types of systems share data related to learners, learning activities, and learning outcomes?

The need to use multiple software systems and applications from different manufacturers together in concert is not unique to the learning profession. In the IT world, this type of multisystem approach is called a service-oriented architecture (SOA). An SOA does not rely on any one vendor or product. It incorporates several networked technologies and platforms from multiple vendors, and it's a lot easier to accomplish when all these systems support a common set of standards. In the learning field, there are two standards organizations addressing this challenge: the IMS Global Learning Consortium® and the Advanced Distributed Learning Initiative.

With the exception of Open Badges, which is described later in this chapter, most of IMS Global's learning systems interoperability standards are geared toward academic K-20 institutions. While many businesses use academic LMS products, they do not tend to use the other types of educational software products used by academia and therefore rarely use these standards. ADL's learning systems interoperability standards are focused on any type of organization that needs to share, track, and store learning data from multiple systems.

IMS Global Learning Consortium Standards

The IMS Global Learning Consortium is a nonprofit organization with members representing K-20 institutions, educational technology providers, educational publishers, government, and professional consortia. The organization has established a collection of specifications to support storing data and content in a standardized way so that it can be moved between many of the leading software-based teaching tools and academic LMS products, reliably and easily.

Academic LMS products require their own kind of interoperability standard. Teachers and instructors who use academic LMS products spend a good deal of valuable time developing course materials, tests, and entire curricula. All that content is locked up inside the LMS, not to mention all of the student records from past and current classes. So what happens when an academic institution wants to switch to a different LMS product? How does it get all that valuable content and data out of the old LMS and into the new one?

If you are a teacher in K-12 or higher education, in addition to an LMS, you may also be using any of a wide variety of educational software products, such as multimedia and video tools, online tutoring and assessment products, off-the-shelf courses and course materials, and digital books. Many of these applications require the same student user accounts, user profiles, and learning history data as that stored in the LMS. Some of these applications generate results like grades and completions that need to be recorded in the LMS transcript. How can data be exchanged between these teaching tools and the LMS? How can the user experience be streamlined so the students don't require multiple, separate logins to the LMS and every teaching tool you use?

The following sections describe eight IMS Global standards relevant to the LMS. The first seven can be found in many academic LMS products. The eighth, Open Badges, can be found in LMS products of all three types: academic, corporate, and LCMS-LMS.

Learning Tools Interoperability® (LTI®)

The IMS Global Learning Tools Interoperability standard allows for the exchange of data between academic LMS products and the content provided by many educational publishers, as well as a wide array of software-based teaching tools. More than 400 educational software products support the LTI standard.

Educational publishers continually update their content, so rather than packaging it up and delivering it to customers, many publishers prefer to maintain their content on their own servers and distribute it to customers over the cloud. Teachers may also use software-based teaching tools to create or assemble content, which must also be presented within the tool in which it was created. In both cases, the LMS must be able to launch the content and track students' use of the content, but it does not actually host the content.

Let's say you are teaching an online college course using an academic LMS. The course materials include interactive content licensed from an educational publisher and interactive exercises you developed using an online multimedia tool. The LMS, publisher's cloud, and multimedia tool are all LTI compliant. LTI hyperlinks and descriptive information are installed on the LMS so that students can identify and launch the content residing in the publisher's cloud and your multimedia tool. As students interact with the content, data are tracked in the cloud and outcomes such as grades or scores are sent back to the LMS. The work done by the LMS, content, and multimedia tool vendors to comply with the LTI specification establishes an out-of-the-box integration between their systems. In this way, LTI allows all the tools you're using to work together seamlessly.

Question & Test Interoperability® (QTI®)

The IMS Global Question & Test Interoperability standard allows for the exchange of data about test items and student results between an academic LMS and other systems that provide assessment content and features.

Let's say you have developed a dozen tests and quizzes in an online tool that your school licensed a few years ago. Students in all your classes have been taking these tests and quizzes. Recently, your school purchased an academic LMS, which supports the same testing features. The school has decided to discontinue licensing the previous product. Does this mean that you will lose the historic student results data? Will you have to redevelop all the tests and quizzes in the new LMS? If both systems are QTI compliant, the test items and student results can be moved from the old tool to the new LMS with relative ease.

OneRoster®

The IMS Global OneRoster standard allows for the exchange of K-12 student profile data between a student information system and an academic LMS. Many K-12 schools use an SIS to keep track of each student's identity, demographic information, and current grade level. Some of this information is also required in the LMS. OneRoster provides a specification for student data to be fed from the SIS to the LMS.

Learning Information Services (LIS)

The IMS Global Learning Information Services standard allows for the exchange of higher education student profile data between an SIS and an academic LMS. While LIS and OneRoster serve a similar purpose, LIS is more focused on the types of student data that are relevant to colleges and universities.

Common Cartridge®

The IMS Global Common Cartridge standard provides a way to package learning content—a single content item or a collection—so that it can be exported from one system and imported into another. Common Cartridge specifies a standard way to aggregate and store the content in a single compressed (zipped) file that contains a manifest, or master index, that identifies the content and defines how it all works together. All systems that support the Common Cartridge standard can import content from the Common Cartridge format, but only some can export content to the Common Cartridge format.

Imagine that your school's license term with its LMS is coming to an end. The school has decided not to renew the license and, instead, implement a new LMS product from a different vendor. You have lots of content in the old LMS, including documents, graphics, presentations, videos, whiteboard drawings, links to content and teaching tools in other systems, and assessments. You spent a lot of time in the old LMS tagging your courses and course materials with metadata pertaining to government curriculum standards. Naturally, you are concerned about how the transition of all this content from the old system to the new one will work out.

First, there have been several versions of the Common Cartridge standard released over the years, so you need to make sure that both LMS products support the same version. If they do, you're in luck. You can export your content from the old LMS to a Common Cartridge format and import it into the new one. Then, you'll be ready to continue with your real job: teaching.

Thin Common Cartridge®

If the Common Cartridge is a barrel, the Thin Common Cartridge standard is a pint-size version. It supports a subset of what the Common Cartridge can do. If all you need to move between systems is LTI links (see the description of Learning Tools Interoperability earlier in this chapter), web links, and metadata, then the Thin Common Cartridge will suffice.

Caliper Analytics®

Analytics are features that enable you to visualize and explore complex data patterns. Analytics should not be confused with reports. The reports produced by an LMS are useful, but they only supply you with data, as in lists of items that can be filtered and sorted. The purpose of reports is to provide you with a readout of the data that have been generated by LMS users. The purpose of analytics is to help you interpret and apply the data.

Data collected from multiple learning tools and systems can become confusing because of the differences in how data are labeled. What one system calls an *answer*, another might call a *selection*, and a third might call a *response.* When you collect these three pieces of data together into a single analytics tool, they appear as different fields even though they are really the same. For analytics to collect data on learning results from multiple systems, a common set of labels is needed.

The IMS Global Caliper Analytics specification provides a standardized method for labeling learning data and measuring learning activities. Software-based teaching tools and academic LMS products that support Caliper are guaranteed to use the same labels, as defined by Caliper, to describe their data. The standard ensures an "apples to apples" view of data from different systems so that you can analyze your complete learning data set in meaningful ways.

Systems that support Caliper have built-in sensors that collect learning activity data. Organizations using Caliper must establish an end point for the data; that is, a single database where the learning activity data are stored. Commercial analytics tools can then be used to visualize and analyze the data.

Open Badges Infrastructure (OBI)

Merit badges have been used by scouting programs for more than 100 years. With achievement comes recognition through a badge that you can sew onto your uniform like a military medal. Badges are used to set goals and motivate the development of new skills and knowledge.

Over the last decade or so, the video game industry has adopted this type of achievement system. Gamers earn points toward a badge, trophy, award, medal, or stamp. A game leaderboard displays the gamer's position in relation to other players.

During that time, there has also been a good deal of research on the linkage between video games, badges, and education. In 2011, the Humanities, Arts, Science, and Technology Advanced Collaboratory introduced an annual digital media and learning competition supported by the MacArthur Foundation to fund innovative badge systems and research studies for education.

Open Badges is a specification created in 2011 by Mozilla and a network of partners. Since that time, the standard has evolved, and the IMS Global Learning Consortium assumed management of the specification in 2017. Unlike other IMS Global standards, which are specific to the academic LMS, Open Badges is supported by many academic, corporate, and LCMS-LMS products.

Mozilla offers a Badge Backpack, which can be used by people to store badges they've earned based on the Open Badges specification. This allows people to take their badges with them from job to job, rather than the badges being locked inside the LMS.

Many LMS products can award badges to learners for completing a course or set of courses, for earning a given number of credits, or in a variety of other ways. If you are interested in using badges in your learning programs, ask your LMS vendor whether the product supports the Open Badges specification, and, if so, how badges are awarded and how they appear in the LMS course catalog and transcript.

Badges representing learning accomplishments and competency mastery may become increasingly important as more academic institutions move toward an evidence-based educational model.

Ask This

Ask your LMS vendor whether the product supports the Open Badges specification, and, if so, how badges are awarded and how they appear in the LMS course catalog and transcript.

Advanced Distributed Learning Initiative Standards

ADL recognizes that many corporate, government, and military organizations need to deliver formal, informal, blended, and workplace learning programs using not just the LMS but also other systems and applications. These learning programs could include content and activities requiring the use of:

- adaptive learning systems
- intelligent tutoring systems
- special purpose simulators
- virtual and augmented reality applications
- wearable technologies
- instructional games
- interactive e-books
- microlearning delivery systems
- knowledge management systems
- performance support systems
- online communities of practice

- analytics tools
- workplace systems.

What has been missing is a set of standards that allows all these systems to share learning-related data. Without these standards, different systems define, track, and store learning-related data, each in its own way, making it very difficult for designers to create learning programs that make cohesive use of multiple systems and applications.

To address the need for learning systems interoperability, ADL provides three key ingredients: the xAPI specification for tracking, processing, and storing learning-related data; the Competency and Skills System (CASS) open source software for managing competencies across multiple systems; and a vision for how to apply those standards, called a total learning architecture.

xAPI

By the mid- to late 2000s, the ADL realized that the SCORM specification was outdated and becoming too limited. SCORM can only track data generated by courses delivered through an LMS. It can only track basic things like page and module completions and test scores. The new reality is that people are learning in many ways outside the LMS—in social networks, online communities, help systems, instructional videos, e-books, mobile apps, and many other platforms. The question became, how can we track any type of learning activity regardless of whether it happens in a course, on an LMS, or anywhere else?

In 2008, the ADL, in collaboration with the Learning Education Training Systems Interoperability organization, engaged the learning and education community for ideas on how to modernize SCORM. In response, the e-learning community contributed more than 200 whitepapers containing a wealth of ideas.

The result is the xAPI specification, which was officially released in April 2013 and has gone through several minor updates since then. Some people still refer to it as *Tin Can,* the project name used during the specification's development. This has led to a good deal of confusion in the field. Its true name is the Experience API, or xAPI for short.

The xAPI specification is based on the concept of tracking activity streams. This is a method used by many popular social media sites. An activity stream is, essentially, a log of the interactions a person has with a site or application, such as visiting a page, typing text, selecting an item from a list, or clicking a button. Activity streams are also able to track the context of each of these interactions. What text did the user type into which field on what page? An activity stream can also roll up a group of interactions into a higher-order activity, such as completing a form or participating in an online discussion.

For example, a social media site might use activity streams to track the topics people visit, along with their posts, replies, and likes. It can then use these data to identify things like the most popular content, the most active users, and topics of interest to specific users. It can even recommend things to users based on their activity data.

The activity stream approach is very flexible. It positions xAPI tracking to be applied in situations that go well beyond SCORM. The xAPI can be used to track data generated by informal workplace learning activities, social media interactions, milestones in games and simulations, and just about any other activity that you can observe or record.

There are three parts to any xAPI solution: activity providers, activity statements, and a learning record store. An activity provider can be any system, software, or app with which a person interacts. An activity statement is a software instruction built into the activity provider that is triggered by a user interaction and records what happened. An LRS, mentioned earlier, is the database that stores the data collected through activity statements. Let's discuss each of these in more detail.

Activity Providers

An activity provider can be an online course, instructional game, simulation, performance support tool, form, video, knowledge base, social network, community of practice, discussion, search tool, website, portal, mobile app, e-book, or any other software you can think of. What makes something an activity provider is that xAPI activity statements have been programmed into it to record what users do, and it has been configured to connect with an LRS, where those user activities will be stored.

Activity Statements

One of the cleverest aspects of xAPI is the construction of the activity statement. Although activity statements are written as programming code, these same activity statements can be communicated by instructional designers to programmers using plain language. This approach enables instructional designers to design xAPI statements needed to track learning activities without knowing anything about programming. An activity statement comprises three parts: a noun, a verb, and an object, as shown in Figure 5-1.

Figure 5-1. xAPI Activity Statement

Learning Record Store

A learning record store is where the resulting xAPI data are stored. It is essentially a database of activity data from all the activity providers with which it is connected. There are a number of commercially available and open source LRS products. A key advantage of the commercial products is the graphical reporting, analytics, and vendor consulting that come with them.

* * *

Let's look at an example of xAPI in action:

Jane is a management trainee who has never written a project proposal. She has a new job where she will be writing lots of project proposals. She must get up to speed quickly so that her company gets new business as a result of the proposals she writes.

Jane's manager is aware that the learning department offers a learning program for people in the organization with similar professional development needs. The learning program involves a combination of formal training and work assignments. It has been reported that 80 percent of employees who completed the learning program generated a winning proposal that earned revenue for the company, so Jane's manager decides to use the learning program.

The learning program starts with formal learning, followed by a set of tasks that Jane completes with coaching from her manager. The company has directed the IT and L&D groups to work together to define and build xAPI statements into the coursework and the employee portal where Jane performs much of her work back on the job. These xAPI statements collect data related to Jane's learning activities and record it in a learning record store. Table 5-1 lists the proposal-writing learning program's xAPI statements. The activity provider is the system that generates the statement and reports it back to the LMS. The learning type column indicates the nature of the activity.

Table 5-1. Examples of Learning Program's xAPI Statements

xAPI Activity Statement	**Activity Provider**	**Learning Type**
Jane completed Proposal Writing Practicum.	Online Course	Formal Learning: Training
Jane passed a test on proposal writing.	Online Assessment	Formal Learning: Evaluation
Jane read a sample project proposal.	Portal (Page Access)	Work Experience: Assignment
Jane attended a meeting about the sample proposal with her manager.	Portal (Calendar)	Work Experience: Coaching and Feedback
Jane created a proposal.	Portal (File Upload)	Work Experience: Assignment
Jane attended a meeting about the proposal with her manager.	Portal (Calendar)	Work Experience: Coaching and Feedback
Jane completed revisions to the proposal.	Portal (File Upload)	Work Experience: Assignment
Jane attended a meeting about the revised proposal with her manager.	Portal (Calendar)	Work Experience: Coaching and Feedback
Jane completed delivering the proposal to a customer.	Portal (File Upload)	Work Experience: Assignment
Jane completed closing the sale.	Portal (CRM Report)	Work Experience: Business Outcome

Foreman (2013f).

At any point, Jane's manager can access a report from the LRS on Jane's progress. After the first two activities, which are formal learning, the remaining statements reflect on-the-job work assignments, coaching, and accomplishments. The xAPI tracks all these statements. Jane was able to learn while producing work outputs and results. This blend of learning and working is a powerful model.

The xAPI specification is just a first piece of a larger ADL initiative called the total learning architecture. A paper resulting from a 2015-2017 ADL research project advocates "the concept of a modern 'learning ecosystem' comprised of interconnected learning opportunities, supported by technology, driven by data, and integrated with other talent management capabilities" (Gallagher et al. 2017).

CASS

ADL's CASS project is open source software that enables multiple systems to share competencies.

Competencies describe the behaviors that are necessary for successful job performance. Let's say your organization has a competency labeled *teamwork.* Four levels of proficiency have been defined for teamwork: novice, baseline, advanced, and expert. What does the teamwork competency look like at each of the proficiency levels? Table 5-2 shows an example of a proficiency scale for the teamwork competency.

Table 5-2. Example Proficiency Scale for the Teamwork Competency

Novice (No Proficiency)	Works independently; does not join in to collaborate with other team members on producing work outputs
Baseline	Collaborates with other team members effectively
Advanced	Collaborates with other team members effectively while engaging less active members and helping the team focus on its goals
Expert	Demonstrates a consistent ability to assemble, organize, and lead teams

These teamwork proficiency levels may be described even more specifically for different job contexts. For example, the observable teamwork behaviors for a sports organization are different from those at a nuclear power plant.

Talent management systems use competencies to create job descriptions, evaluate job applicants, match strategic goals to workforce capabilities, develop business leaders, and more. Corporate LMS products use competencies to create learning paths, identify courses to address competency gaps, and so on. The problem is that each system has its own way of handling competencies. Some have a single list of competencies, while others contain competency menus and submenus. In some, an individual either has a competency or doesn't, while in others, a competency can be performed at different levels of proficiency. Some can describe a single competency in a variety of ways, based on the job or work context. These differences make competency data difficult to share across systems.

CASS solves these problems. It consists of three components: competency portability, competency reporting, and resource alignment. As CASS development matures, LMS products and other learning systems may take advantage of its capabilities by embedding or providing an out-of-the-box integration with the CASS software.

Competency Portability

Competency portability allows multiple systems, including an LMS, to share competencies even if the competency structures differ. It does this by providing a method to associate competencies in one model with competencies in another. A competency in one system can be identified as "the same as" or "related to" a competency in another system. Rubrics can be configured to determine whether several detailed competencies are equivalent to a single higher-level competency or whether having a higher-level competency means that you also have lower-level competencies. If the systems you are using do not have competencies at all, you can use CASS as a competency repository that other systems can access.

Competency Reporting

Competency reporting allows you to define "assertions" that a person has a competency. An assertion can be a certificate or badge, sign-off by an authorized observer or supervisor, or a set of xAPI statements that provide evidence of a person's competency. A competency assertion can be configured to expire after a specified amount of time. For example, competence at administering CPR may need to be reinforced, refreshed, and reasserted periodically. A competency assertion can also be configured to decay over a given timeframe. For example, competency at marathon running may decay without maintaining good health and proper physical conditioning. An assertion can be limited by certain conditions. For example, competency at driving an automobile safely may be asserted for fair and mildly inclement weather, but not for torrential rain or snowstorm conditions.

Resource Alignment

Resource alignment is the association between a piece of content and a competency. Each competency-content association has a set of properties that name and describe the content, the learning program to which the content belongs, the URL to access the content, and an alignment type, which indicates whether the content assesses, teaches, or requires the competency.

Total Learning Architecture

The total learning architecture is a vision for how ADL standards can be applied to liberate learning design from the constraint of traditional courses and move beyond the LMS to incorporate multiple systems and applications in the learning experience.

The vision includes four types of data that systems will need to share in support of learning: learning evidence, competencies, learning context, and learner profiles.

Learning Evidence

Learning evidence proves that a person learned something they didn't know before (a learning outcome) or can do something they couldn't do before (a performance outcome). A traditional course may provide evidence of a learning outcome in the form of a passing test score. ADL's vision allows for many more ways to collect learning evidence. For example, the subject completed all the steps in the proper order, performed a task or procedure within a specific amount of time, delivered a work product, was observed performing effectively, received supervisor sign-off on a specific deliverable or accomplishment, or some combination of these.

After an instructional designer identifies the intended learning and performance outcomes for a learning program, they must determine what, how, when, and from where to collect evidence of those outcomes. Due to its flexible and open structure, xAPI can be used to track evidence of learning and performance, whether it happens in the LMS or in another system or application.

Competencies

As mentioned earlier, competencies describe the behaviors that are necessary for successful job performance. Organizations use competencies to describe what is required to be effective in a job role or work assignment, allowing them to assess a person's current competencies and competency gaps. Learning programs can focus on the participant's acquisition of specific competencies. This approach has potential for developing employees in ways that benefit the organization strategically.

The ADL CASS specification can be used to link different systems to a common set of competencies, keep track of associations between competencies and learning content, and define the learning evidence that asserts a person has acquired a competency.

Learning Context

In ADL's vision for a total learning architecture, learning context data will enable learning systems to detect information about a learner for use in recommending and personalizing learning content. This may include situational information about how the user is accessing the content, such as the time of day, location, device used, and connection type; user profile information, such as the user's job, preferred language, and preferred delivery method; and user history information, such as learning credits, certifications, badges, and competency assertions. Future ADL standards will support this approach.

Learner Profiles

Learner profiles include the kind of information you might find in any system's user profile, but the ADL vision goes a step further. In the total learning architecture, learner profiles will list the competencies a user has and those the user needs based on the learning context. This information can be used to develop and monitor progress in personalized development plans.

The ADL standards allow for a more engaging, relevant, and personalized user experience. For the learner, these specifications will enable personal learning and development achievements and records to be taken from one school or employer to another. For the instructional designer, these specifications promise to liberate learning design by enabling designers to incorporate multiple technologies into a learning program, knowing that the relevant data are shared and accumulated across platforms. For the chief learning officer, the notion that the LMS is the central and sole repository for what is now a relatively limited set of course-specific learning data will give way to a more comprehensive set of learning data that are stored in a way that can be shared across many systems.

Accessibility

Now that we've covered interoperability standards, let's move on to another standard that is important to the LMS: accessibility.

A system's compliance with accessibility standards is important to all organizations, and it is the law for many government agencies. Accessibility standards make software applications usable to more people with visual, physical, auditory, and cognitive challenges. These standards work in conjunction with assistive devices such as screen readers, voice control, and switch controls.

Many people with visual challenges or blindness rely on screen readers to use software. A screen reader recites the text and interaction options on the page. For a screen reader to make any sense of pictures, photos, icons, logos, and other graphics, the images must include a descriptive text-based label. Image labels can be entered in HTML, but many times software developers, who may not be aware of their value to screen readers, don't enter them.

Another visual challenge involves color blindness. Designers who use color to organize information or interactions should simultaneously use other methods and not rely on color alone.

In addition, many people unable to use a mouse or joystick due to visual, physical, or cognitive limitations often use a voice control or switch control that emulates a keyboard. For software to support these controls, keystroke alternatives to "mousing" must be available.

The two most prevalent accessibility standards are Section 508 of the U.S. government's Rehabilitation Act, which requires federal agencies to make digital systems and information accessible to employees and citizens with disabilities, and the Web Content Accessibility Guidelines (WCAG) published by the international Internet standards organization, the World Wide Web Consortium (WC3).

Web Content Accessibility Guidelines

The initial version of the standard, WCAG 1.0, was first published in 1999. The current version is WCAG 2.0, published in 2008. It includes 12 guidelines, each with a set of criteria that can be tested to ensure compliance. WC3 has also published a set of techniques that web designers and developers can use to apply the guidelines.

In 2012, WCAG 2.0 was adopted by the International Organization for Standardization and published as ISO/IEC 40500:2012.

If you are interested in testing the accessibility compliance of your LMS, there are a number of third-party organizations that offer WCAG 2.0 audits and site reports.

Section 508

In the United States, legislation to prevent discrimination against people with disabilities in the federal workforce dates back to the end of World War I. Over the years, the legislation evolved in many positive ways until the 1960s, when it was expanded beyond people with physical and mental disabilities to provide assistance to a broader range of people who had trouble finding jobs due to things like alcoholism, drug abuse, and serving time in jail. This expansion arguably made the legislation untenable, too broad-based and complex for compliance and enforcement to be managed.

In 1973, the United States introduced an entirely new Rehabilitation Act focused on protecting the rights of and preventing discrimination against people with physical and mental disabilities who wanted to work in federal jobs, for federally funded programs, and in jobs with federal contractors. In the years since its introduction, the Rehabilitation Act has been amended to address issues people with disabilities face beyond employment, such as community inclusion and consumer protections.

Section 508 was enacted in a 1998 amendment to the Rehabilitation Act of 1973. It mandates that all information technology developed and used by the federal government be accessible to people with disabilities. While there is no official certification of Section 508 compliance, some private organizations and trade associations provide product accessibility templates to assist software vendors in assessing the compliance of their products.

Security and Privacy

In any data system, security and privacy are two separate but related issues. Security is focused on preventing unauthorized access to a system and its data. The ability for a hacker to access a system and steal its data results from a problem with the system's security. To secure a system, you or your vendor must configure a number of system parameters that protect access to the system and its data.

> **LMS Accessibility Considerations**
>
> Some systems comply with these standards more fully than others. If you need to know whether your LMS is Section 508 or WCAG compliant, there are three key questions to consider:
>
> **How compliant is it?**
>
> One LMS may be more or less compliant than another. Ask your LMS vendor to list the specific features of the product that make it compatible with assistive devices such as screen readers, voice control, and switch controls. Ask your vendor to provide a list of the WCAG guidelines with which the LMS is complaint.
>
> **How much of the system is compliant?**
>
> Some LMS products may offer compliance features in the general user interface but lack those features in the administrator interface. Ask your vendor about this.
>
> **Is there evidence of compliance?**
>
> Having customers in the U.S. federal government is a good indicator of an LMS product vendor's Section 508 compliance. Ask your vendor to provide the contacts of any federal agency customers.

Privacy is focused on how the user data collected in a system are used. A company that shares the contact information and buying habits of its customers with other companies is not keeping its customer data private. To protect the privacy of your users, you must establish, communicate, and enforce a policy on how the data collected in the system will be used.

Standard Security Controls

To keep a system secure, you must require users to log in and be authenticated before they can access the system's data and features. After login, the specific features and data that each user can access are controlled by roles and permissions. Make sure there are no potential back doors into the system.

Sensitive data such as passwords or credit card information must be encrypted if they are stored in the system's database. Better yet, avoid the permanent storage of credit card information and instead require users to enter the information each time they pay for a course.

To protect sensitive data when they are transmitted from the user to the LMS through the Internet, the data should be encrypted using Secure Sockets Layer. When data transmission is secured, the user will see *https://* instead of *http://* in the LMS web address.

International Organization for Standardization

The International Organization for Standardization (ISO) comprises standards groups from more than 160 nations. ISO standards contain clear criteria that can be proven and certified. While many LMS vendors have not been ISO certified, those that are instill in their customers a greater sense of confidence. Some organizations even require that their information system providers be ISO certified. Ask your LMS vendor whether they are certified in the following ISO standards.

ISO 27001

LMS vendors operating in the cloud and third-party hosting services are ultimately responsible for the security of your data. This ISO standard specifies what is required for a hosting provider to establish and maintain a systematic approach to managing information security.

ISO 9001

ISO 9001 is a widely adopted standard that specifies what is required for establishing and maintaining a systematic approach to managing quality. If your vendor is ISO 9001 certified, you can be confident that your LMS meets the needs of its customers while also complying with statutory and regulatory requirements.

Government Agency Security Controls

Government agencies using an LMS may have additional security requirements. In the United States, the security of systems used by federal government employees is governed by the Federal Information Security Management Act (FISMA) of 2002. Security requirements for cloud-based solutions may need to be certified through the Federal Risk and Authorization Management Program (FedRAMP), which assigns a security impact level of low, moderate, or high to the LMS and uses specific tests to measure whether it meets the criteria of its assigned impact level. LMS implementations in the U.S. Department of Defense may need to be certified in the DoD Information Assurance Certification and Accreditation Process (DIACAP) to ensure system security risks are managed appropriately.

No matter where you are in the world, if you're responsible for a government agency's LMS, check with your vendor to determine what experience they have with other customers in your country's government and if they have already been through the required security certification processes.

Ask This

Ask your vendor what experience they have with other customers in your country's government and whether they've been through the required security certification processes.

Country-Specific Privacy Laws

Be sure your LMS is compliant with the privacy laws of the countries in which your users are located. Some countries have established strict laws related to data privacy. Failure to comply with these laws can result in penalties. For example, the Ministry of Industry and Information Technology in China has issued cybersecurity laws that address data privacy; France has long-standing data protection laws that are enforced by the Commission Nationale de l'Informatique et des Libertés; Germany's Bundesdatenschutzgesetz regulates personal data in information technology systems; and in Sweden, the Electronic Communications Act and Personal Data Act regulate data privacy. Check with your IT organization and legal department for guidance on what you need to consider, and then work with your LMS vendor to make sure the LMS is configured to comply with the data privacy laws of the countries in which your organization operates.

LMS administrators and IT professionals are sometimes unaware of data privacy risks and concerns. Professional associations such as the International Association of Privacy Professionals provide training and certification programs related to the effective management of data privacy.

Key Takeaways

This chapter explained the various standards and specifications used to make your content and corporate or academic LMS work well together; ensure your system is accessible to people with visual, physical, auditory, and cognitive challenges; keep your system secure; and maintain the privacy of your user's data. The key takeaways are:

- Three corporate LMS interoperability specifications ensure your e-learning courseware works properly with your LMS: AICC, SCORM, and cmi5.

- A collection of academic LMS interoperability specifications ensures your online content, teaching tools, and LMS can exchange data: Learning Tools Interoperability, Question & Test Interoperability, OneRoster, Learning Information Services, Common Cartridge, Thin Common Cartridge, Caliper Analytics, and Open Badges.
- Three standards support data sharing among the various learning technologies, including the LMS, used in business, government, and professional associations: the xAPI specification, the Competency and Skills System, and the vision for a total learning architecture.
- Accessibility standards like Web Content Accessibility Guidelines and Section 508 work with assistive devices to make software applications usable to more people with visual, physical, auditory, and cognitive challenges.
- Security and data privacy are key concerns for any information system, including your LMS.

This concludes part 1, which was focused on explaining the various types of LMS products and their features, relevant standards, and specifications. Part 2 focuses on how to select, implement, and operate an LMS.

PART 2

How to Select, Implement, and Operate an LMS

CHAPTER 6

Selecting the Right LMS for Your Organization

This chapter introduces a proven process for evaluating and selecting an LMS. It explains how to analyze your needs, define requirements, focus on the right products, evaluate how those products meet your requirements, and select the right LMS for you. It also discusses negotiation and contracting with the LMS vendor.

If you don't have an LMS, or you use a product that has not been upgraded for several years, your organization may be missing some beneficial features that are available in current products. If you already have an LMS and are not satisfied with its features and capabilities, it may be time to consider a more suitable product. The LMS marketplace is always changing, with new players emerging all the time. A product that is well suited to your organization's needs is probably out there.

Finding the LMS that best meets your organization's needs is not easy. Hundreds of LMS products are available. An organization's investment in an LMS and related technologies is considerable, both financially and in the time spent choosing one. All this combines to heighten the possible risk of selecting the wrong solution. LMS implementation can involve a significant disruption to your organization. Once the LMS is in place, your organization is likely to use it for the next three to five years, or more. You certainly don't want to pour your efforts into a product poorly matched to your needs.

A study I conducted with the eLearning Guild showed that the process an organization uses to evaluate and select an LMS can have a significant impact on an organization's satisfaction with the solution (Foreman 2013a). Figure 6-1 shows that, of survey respondents who thought that their evaluation and selection process was ineffective, less than one quarter are satisfied with their LMS product. As the respondents' view of their evaluation process's effectiveness increases, so does their satisfaction with the LMS product.

Figure 6-1. Satisfaction With the LMS by Effectiveness of Prepurchase Evaluation and Selection Process

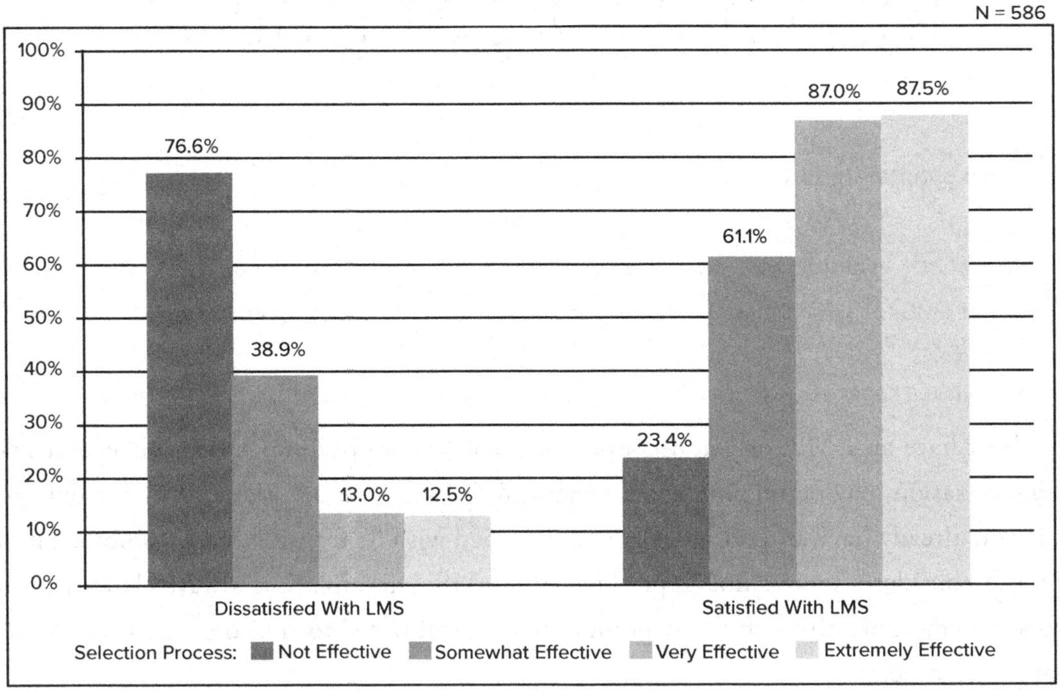

Adapted from Foreman (2013a) with permission from the eLearning Guild.

So, if your organization wants to evaluate LMS products and vendors effectively—and come away satisfied with the decision—what should you do?

How to Evaluate Products and Select an LMS

LMS evaluation and selection is a process that involves five major steps, as shown in Figure 6-2: Analyze your needs, define your requirements, vet products, evaluate suitable products, and select a product. These steps reflect a proven practice for LMS evaluation and selection. Although this process may take more time and effort than you anticipated, it helps ensure that you end up with an LMS that is best suited to your needs. Ultimately, following this process will save you from wasting valuable time, money, effort, and sponsorship support on a failed LMS project.

Figure 6-2. LMS Evaluation and Selection Process Steps

Step 1: Analyze Needs

Your first step is to analyze the needs of your organization. Without a needs analysis, you can only make assumptions about what your organization really needs from an LMS. Your assumptions are likely to be based on your perspective and, perhaps, those of the people you work with most closely. I have seen groups start listing features they want in an LMS without giving much thought to the needs of other key stakeholders. This "head in the sand" approach can result in a solution that meets some of the organization's needs—but not all. It is critical that you ask others in the organization what they need to manage learning. By exploring the perspectives of your stakeholders, you are likely to discover important needs that you would not have identified on your own.

There are other benefits to this approach. You will be connecting with your users to gather input that will inform your LMS selection and may also help you better align your training strategy, initiatives, and priorities with those of the organization. People who are involved in evaluation activities tend to have more ownership of the resulting decision and become acclimated to the product in advance of implementation. Your sponsors will have increased confidence in the decision because of the due diligence involved in the process. Through this evaluation process, the learning organization builds relationships with its customers, sponsors, stakeholders, and IT, all of which help set the stage for implementation.

You will need to start by identifying and talking with stakeholders. These are the people in your organization who will be affected by the new LMS. Some of your key stakeholders are people in leadership and management roles, who are concerned with ensuring the people in their departments have the needed skills and knowledge to be productive. Other stakeholders include people who will use the LMS, such as e-learning developers, training schedulers, instructors, registrars, and data analysts. You may not be able to speak with every single stakeholder; a representative sample from each key group will be fine. Your goal for these discussions is to collect data that reflect the entire organization's needs and goals so that you can define a comprehensive set of requirements that your LMS must meet.

So, what is a requirement? Requirements describe the capabilities the LMS must have to be useful to your organization. Your requirements should cover all aspects of what all your stakeholder groups need. LMS requirements are similar to course learning objectives. They describe what you need to be able to do once you have the LMS.

Explore the Leadership View

People in leadership roles are likely to provide a strategic point of view. Whenever possible, start here. Awareness of the strategy informs some of the more tactical and technical questions that should be explored with management later in the analysis process.

Contact these leaders and let them know that you seek a strategic viewpoint as part of the needs analysis you are conducting for purchasing an enterprise LMS. To gain the most information you can in a short amount of time, you will want to meet one-on-one with each leader. Ask for a 20- to 30-minute interview.

When you sit down with the leader, ask the big, open-ended questions like, "What do you see as the key human performance challenges for our organization over the next three to five years?" You may be surprised at how much useful information and insight leaders will share, from which you can form LMS requirements.

For example, I once met with the chief financial officer of a $12 billion company and asked two questions: "What are the key strategic goals of the company over the next several years, and what do you see as the most critical human performance challenges related to achieving those goals?" He responded that the company was expecting rapid global growth through mergers and acquisitions. This would require the effective assimilation of people from other companies, who spoke different languages and were accustomed to different corporate cultures, business processes, systems, and tools.

I then met with several executive vice presidents who expressed concern about the company's need to meet the regulatory compliance requirements of all the countries in which it manufactured and sold its products. One emphasized her belief that although English tends to be the primary language in which global business was conducted at the company, people need to be given the opportunity to *learn* in their native language.

This collection of leadership viewpoints generated a set of strategic drivers for LMS requirements. The drivers were global growth, regulatory compliance, and a need to learn in one's native language. These strategic goals drove requirements for multilingual support; tracking, reporting, and management of compliance training and retraining; and coordination with human resources on the timing and processes for adding acquired employee groups to the human resource management system, which would share data with the LMS.

Explore the Management View

Your next step is to meet with middle management and other key stakeholders. People in management roles are likely to provide an operational point of view. This group should include managers of people in each of the departments and functional areas that will use the LMS to get training. Other key stakeholders may include people in satellite training groups, such as customer training, supplier training, sales training, or regional training.

I like to meet with managers in focus groups. I find that groups of managers tend to react to one another's comments. When a single manager brings up an issue and no one responds, I make a note and move on. When a manager brings up an issue and a lively group discussion ensues, I know I've found a concern that is more broadly experienced and therefore carries more weight.

When organizing focus groups, I suggest selecting managers at the same management level in similar functional areas. Mixing higher- and lower-level managers in the same group can result in some people not wanting to speak up and risk judgment by their supervisors or subordinates. Mixing functional areas can create a lack of focus. Managers from one area may dominate parts of the conversation, which the other functions may find irrelevant.

I subscribe to a few additional guiding rules for assembling focus groups. First, plan for just enough time to gather all the data you need. I find that 60 to 90 minutes is usually sufficient. Second, keep the group size manageable to ensure that everyone has a chance to speak. I prefer a size of eight to 12 people. Third, bring a colleague to help conduct the discussion and share the note-taking. You need to capture the salient information that is discussed, while steering the conversation, pursuing issues, and knowing when to move on. A colleague can help by picking up lines of questioning, hearing things, and taking notes that you may have missed. If you cannot find a colleague to help you, consider bringing a recorder to minimize your note-taking so that you can focus on leading the discussion. Finally, do not bring so many colleagues that you outnumber the people in the focus group. Doing so can be quite intimidating to focus group participants.

If you are planning to replace your current LMS, you might want to kick off the discussion by asking people what they like most about the current solution and what they would most like to see improved. If your organization is starting this process for the first time, focus your questions on how learning is managed currently and the key problems areas—operationally and financially.

Explore the IT View

When you meet with people from IT, you may find that a number of discussions need to take place. First, IT has its own training needs and, in that sense, will be an end user of the LMS. Second, and perhaps more important, IT is tasked with managing the organization's technology infrastructure, so they are likely to be concerned about how the LMS will fit into the broader IT architecture and what technical support will be required of them.

Consider exploring these two IT perspectives in separate focus groups. For IT's training needs, you will need to speak with the IT people who are responsible for training. This discussion will be similar to those you had in the management focus groups.

The IT infrastructure discussion will be focused on the technical standards, processes, and constraints that will drive your LMS technology requirements. This discussion will encompass IT's strategy related to cloud-based solutions, mobile access, network demand, security, privacy, systems integration, scalability, reliability, and support. From this discussion, you will generate a set of technical requirements. Consider including someone from your team or a consultant who understands the technical side of the LMS and is well acquainted with the perspective and typical concerns of IT.

When Are You Done With the Needs Analysis?

A rule of thumb is to keep meeting with people until you start to get mostly repetitive information. Once you have collected sufficient input from the interviews and focus groups, you should be able to identify strategic, operational, and technical drivers from which you can define your LMS requirements. Table 6-1 lists some examples.

Table 6-1. Examples of Strategic, Operational, and Technical Drivers

Driver	Example
Strategic Driver	Your leadership states that your organization is behind the competition in offering quality training to its customers on how to use its products.
Operational Driver	Managers in the customer service division tell you that they would really like to map learning programs with their key performance indicators so that they can prescribe the right training to the right people.
Operational Driver	Some of your training managers mention that delays of a day or more in updating learning records for training delivered halfway around the world have been causing problems with report accuracy.
Technical Driver	Your IT department stresses the need for any new system to meet the enterprise security, accessibility, and data privacy standards they have established.

The strategic, operational, and technical drivers you discover during needs analysis will bring your LMS needs and requirements into focus. This approach will ensure that your LMS selection criteria are in alignment with your organization's goals and priorities.

Step 2: Define Requirements

Requirements form the basis of your LMS selection criteria. The clearer and more complete your LMS requirements, the easier it is to evaluate products. Try to focus on what learners or administrators must be able to do with the LMS.

When writing requirements, keep in mind that LMS vendors will need to accurately interpret each requirement to respond to it or demonstrate that it can be met by their product. Even more important, you will need to test and verify that the products you're considering can meet each requirement.

There are four rules to follow when writing LMS requirements:

1. **Write your requirements clearly and unambiguously.** Table 6-2 lists some examples of requirements that are stated ambiguously, explains why they are a problem, and shows how they can be rewritten more clearly.

Table 6-2. Examples of Requirements Written Ambiguously and Unambiguously

Ambiguously Written Requirement	Problem	Unambiguously Written Requirement
The LMS must be accessible by commonly used mobile devices without excessive horizontal scrolling.	The LMS vendor must decide which mobile devices are commonly used and how much horizontal scrolling is excessive.	The LMS user interface must support responsive web design and be accessible on the most recent three versions of all iOS and Android devices.
The LMS must enable authorized administrators to create and maintain curricula made up of one or more courses, including but not limited to instructor-led classes, virtual classes, e-learning courses, and assessments.	Terms such as *not limited to* make it difficult to verify that a requirement has been met.	The LMS must enable authorized administrators to create and maintain curricula made up of one or more courses, including instructor-led classes, virtual classes, e-learning courses, and assessments.
The LMS must enable learners to easily identify and access courses that have been assigned to them.	Subjective terms, such as *easily* or *quickly* and most other adverbs, make it difficult to verify that a requirement has been met.	The LMS must enable learners to identify and access courses that have been assigned to them.

2. **Make sure each requirement is discrete and does not repeat or overlap with other requirements.**

3. **Express each requirement as a need, not a solution.** Table 6-3 shows an example of a requirement that is expressed as a solution, describes why it is a problem, and shows how the requirement can be rewritten as a need.

Table 6-3. Example Requirement Expressed as a Solution Versus a Need

Requirement Expressed as a Solution	Problem	Requirement Expressed as a Need
The LMS must provide a link on the homepage where a user can change languages to any of the following . . . *(list of languages)*	Because you have stated that the language selector must be a link on the homepage, this requirement would limit your vendors from providing the option to select a language in the user profile or in a drop-down list on the homepage.	The LMS user interface must support the following languages . . . *(list of languages)*

4. **Try to write all requirements at the same level of detail.** If you end up with somewhere between 30 and 60 requirements, you're probably at the right level of detail. I have seen organizations generate a list of 300 or 400 requirements; some inadequately described a broad set of functionality, and others were too detailed and did not fully describe the need.

Sometimes it helps to organize your requirements into categories, such as functional and technical. Functional requirements describe what the system must be able to do from a learning management perspective, whereas technical requirements describe how the system must fit into the broader IT enterprise infrastructure. Table 6-4 lists some examples of requirements in each of these two categories.

You can also define subcategories under each of the two general categories. For example, under functional requirements, you might use administration, general course management, classroom learning management, online learning management, personalization, navigation, enrollment, and learning results as subcategories. Under technical requirements, you might list online learning interoperability, accessibility and security, systems integration, and system performance and management.

Table 6-4. Examples of Functional and Technical Requirements

Functional Requirements	Technical Requirements
• The LMS must support the delivery of training to employees and customers. • The LMS must provide a way for courses and content to be associated with key performance indicators. • The LMS must provide a way to search on a key performance indicator to find relevant courses and content. • The LMS must segment regional data in reports and provide a date and time stamp for the data reported in each region.	• The LMS must restrict access to courses and content that should not be seen by customers. • The LMS user interface must conform to Web Content Accessibility Guidelines and U.S. Section 508 standards. • The LMS must comply with Germany's Bundesdatenschutzgesetz data protection act.

It is important to prioritize your requirements. By prioritizing your requirements, you can use a weighted scorecard to evaluate how well various LMS products meet each requirement and then calculate overall scores that indicate which products align best with your requirements and priorities. Some organizations use a simple method for prioritizing requirements, like high, medium, and low. I prefer to use a statistical approach called analytic hierarchy process (AHP), which assigns a weight to each requirement, because its results reflect priorities more accurately. AHP identifies the importance of each requirement compared with other requirements and assigns it a weight. AHP is very effective when used with a group of people because it drives discussion, consensus, and a shared vision of what features are most important and what the organization can expect from an LMS. A web search on AHP will provide lots of additional information and even some Excel templates, which you can customize for use in your LMS project.

Step 3: Vet Products

Once you've analyzed your needs and defined your requirements, your challenge is to narrow the hundreds of LMS choices to a short list of products. To get started, decide which of the three major types of LMS products will be your focus: corporate LMS, academic LMS, or LCMS-LMS. Then, decide whether you need a stand-alone LMS or an app or plug-in for your existing WordPress, Salesforce, or SharePoint sites. Consider whether you want to explore LMS products that specialize in your industry, or broaden your search for products to encompass more general-purpose solutions.

Next, identify eight to 10 requirements that can help you rule out nonqualifying products. For example, not all LMS products support multiple languages. If this requirement is critical for your organization, then it is a good vetting criterion. Not all products comply with specific accessibility and security regulations. Some LMS products support online courses only. Others support instructor-led, but not online. Some have e-commerce features, and some do not. Some support SCORM; others do not. Some support cmi5, while others do not. These can all be good vetting criteria.

Once you have defined a set of vetting criteria, you can research product websites and contact vendors to inquire about their product's support for your vetting criteria. Select a short list of products, perhaps eight to 12 that meet all or most of your vetting criteria. This gives you a manageable number of products to evaluate in more detail without being overwhelmed.

Step 4: Evaluate Products

The product evaluation process works like a funnel, as shown in Figure 6-3. With each evaluation activity, you rule out nonqualifying products and continue to evaluate those that best meet your requirements. The list of products you are considering gets smaller as you complete each evaluation activity.

You will need to find the appropriate balance between thoroughness and efficiency. I have found that the following evaluation activities yield optimum results. The first two activities—request for information (RFI) and use case demonstrations—should be performed in order. Activities 3 through 6—trial version, IT review, customer referrals, and vendor health—can be performed concurrently. Activity 7, request for proposal (RFP), should be last. However, I have at times streamlined this process by combining or omitting some of the activities when working with organizations with time or logistical constraints.

Figure 6-3. LMS Evaluation Activities

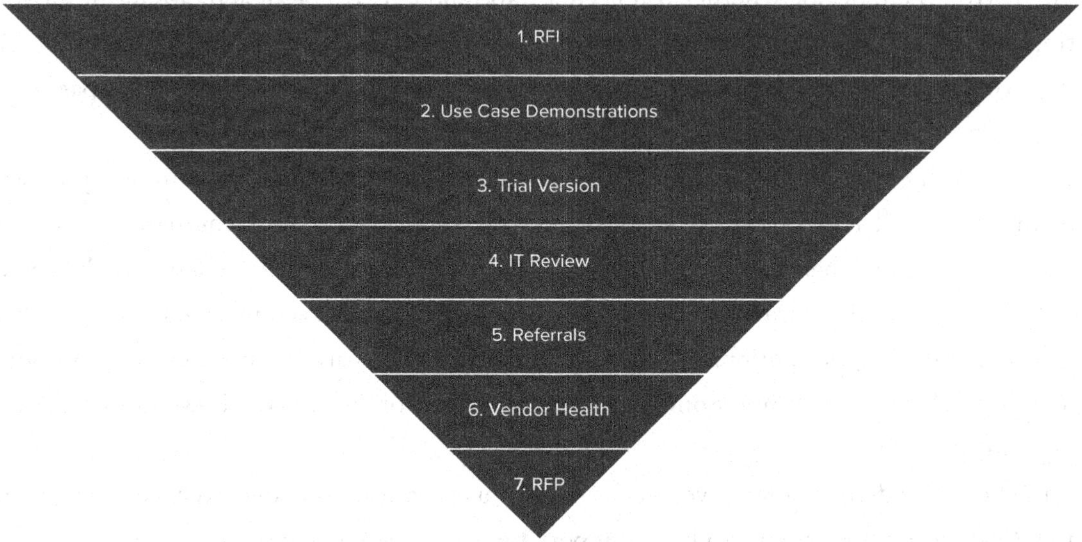

Foreman (2013b).

Request for Information

A good activity to start with is an RFI. It contains all your requirements, with two to six questions per requirement for vendors to answer. Avoid asking yes or no questions; ask open-ended questions that will require vendors to describe how they meet the requirement. For example, instead of asking the vendor, "Can your product provide a report on enrollments?" ask the vendor, "Please describe your product's reporting capabilities, and include a list of all available reports."

The vendors' written responses to your RFI provide valuable information that will help you gain insight into their products, their ability to interpret your requirements, and their responsiveness to your requests. It is a great way to gain an in-depth view of the capabilities of the products you are considering, outside the context of the vendor's typical sales process.

When you've put together your RFI document, contact your vetted list of vendors. Let them know that you are in the process of evaluating and selecting an LMS and that you have selected their product as a candidate. Ask if they are willing to respond to an RFI. If not, they do not value your business enough to invest the time. This is a strong indicator that they will not view you as a high-priority customer and may be difficult to work with. Cross them off the list and move on. If they agree, send them the RFI along with a due date for their response.

You may need to set ground rules to keep the process fair for all vendors. For example, you may decide that no vendor will be told who the other vendors are, answers to any questions asked by one vendor will be distributed to all vendors, and no RFI responses will be accepted after the due date.

Decide who in your organization will be involved in reviewing and scoring RFI responses. Depending on the number of requirements, it may take one to three hours to evaluate each vendor's response. It is important that all reviewers agree to review all the vendor responses. Using different reviewers for different vendors, or accepting a reviewer's evaluation of some of the vendors but not all, will skew your results. This would be unfair to the vendors, who have put a good deal of time and effort into responding to the RFI. More important, it would be counter-productive to your LMS evaluation and selection efforts.

Provide a scorecard for reviewers to use as they evaluate the vendor responses. The scorecard should allow reviewers to rate how well the vendor meets each requirement. I like to use a five-point scale, such as unsatisfactory, suboptimal, acceptable, strong, and optimal. Table 6-5 shows an example of an RFI scorecard.

Table 6-5. Example of an RFI Scorecard

Scoring Key: 1-Unsatisfactory; 2-Suboptimal; 3-Acceptable; 4-Strong; 5-Optimal				
	LMS 1	LMS 2	LMS 3	Etc.
Requirement 1				
Requirement 2				
Requirement 3				
Etc.				

When reviewing an RFI response, focus on one requirement at a time. Read the vendor's responses to each question related to the requirement and rate the product based on what you read. Ideally, the vendor responses should be clear, concise, thorough, and pertinent. However, keep in mind that you are not rating the vendor's grammar or writing style. You are rating how well the vendor's product matches up with the requirement, based on what you have read.

Once all the reviewers have completed their scorecards, you can aggregate the scores to calculate an average score for each requirement, for each vendor. If you have applied weights to prioritize the requirements, you can incorporate the weight into the score for each requirement. You can then total the scores for each requirement category and subcategory, as well as a single, overall score. These scores will reflect how well each of the LMS products matches up with your requirements, based on what is most important to your organization.

After scoring the responses to the RFI, you can rule out some of the lower-scoring vendors and continue evaluating the top contenders. Send a message to the vendors you plan to drop from consideration while thanking them for their RFI responses. Let them know that despite its strengths their product did not match up with your requirements as well as some of the others you reviewed.

Use Case Demonstrations

Meet with your review team to brainstorm a list of 10 or 12 use cases. A use case is a scenario or goal and set of parameters that would typically be performed by a learner or administrator. Use cases should reflect the way your organization manages learning. Select some common use cases as well as some that are complex and challenging. This will enable you to compare all vendors based on the same demonstration criteria.

Next, ask the vendor to demonstrate some of your common use cases. These might include scheduling training events, administering annual compliance training, finding and registering for a course, or generating an important report.

Ask This

Ask the vendor to demonstrate some of your common use cases.

Don't stop there. Go beyond the common scenarios and think about some of the trickier things you may need. I worked with an organization that offered an instructor-led course that took place over a three-week timeframe with a "checkerboard" schedule. A class would meet in week one on Monday from 8 a.m. to 12 p.m., and on Thursday from 1 to 5 p.m. at a different location with a different instructor. The sessions on weeks two and three met on different days and times. This was a very good use case to try with LMS vendors. The sidebar shows an example of how you might document a use case for your vendors to demonstrate.

Use Case: Create a Learning Path

Background: A learning path is provided for each key function in our organization. It consists of a number of learning requirements, each of which is supported by one or more classes, materials, and assessments. An individual requirement within a learning path may have an expiration date, upon which the learner must refresh their skills by completing the most recent learning activities to fulfill the learning requirement.

Demonstration: Please demonstrate how a learning path can be created in your product.

Instructions: Create a learning path mapped to a particular role or function. The learning path should contain at least four learning requirements, which must be taken in an enforced sequence. The first learning requirement is met by completing an instructor-led class. The second learning requirement is met by accessing a document containing policies and performance standards and getting electronic signature sign-off from your mentor that you have reviewed the materials and met with your mentor to discuss them. The third learning requirement is completed by achieving a passing score of at least 80 percent in an online assessment. The fourth learning requirement is completed by fulfilling the criteria of an in situ observation by your mentor. The learner must complete all four learning requirements within three months to get credit for completing the learning path. The second learning requirement is set to expire and requires retraining annually.

Invite each of the top contenders to meet with your organization, either physically or virtually, to demonstrate how their product handles each use case. Send the use cases to the vendors in advance so that they can prepare. Let them know that their demonstrations will be evaluated by the attendees and compared with demos from other vendors. Some vendors will want to spend time giving you a sales presentation telling you about their customer base, market share, history, and so on. I like to allow the vendors to manage their use of the allotted time, but emphasize that the meeting will end on time, they must demonstrate all the use cases, and they must clearly state to participants which use case they are demonstrating.

Again, you can distribute a scorecard to participants so they can evaluate the vendor demonstrations. Tally the scores and rule out those vendors whose products did not perform well in the demonstrations. At this point, you should have a short list of qualified "finalist" products.

Trial Version

As you continue to evaluate the finalists, you may ask each of the vendors for a trial version of the LMS software or access to a "sandbox" installation in the cloud where you can explore the product. Hands-on exploration will give you a better sense of the user interface design, features, and capabilities of the product.

Invite members of the review team, learning management administrators, people who need to run reports, and others who will use the LMS directly and frequently, to try out the product. Set a date and time to meet with the reviewers to discuss their experiences with and opinions of each product. Use a flipchart to list positives and negatives for each product. Decide whether any of the products should be dropped from consideration.

Ask This

Ask each of the vendors for a trial version of the LMS software or access to a "sandbox" installation in the cloud where you can explore the product.

IT Review

Set up one or two meetings between your vendor's technical staff and your IT organization for some "under-the-hood" discussions. The purpose of these discussions will be to satisfy IT that the vendor's technology, security, and integration capabilities are acceptable; set the vendor's expectations about what will be required, technically, to implement their product in your organization; and establish a professional rapport between the vendor and your IT team, which will benefit your organization later if you decide to implement the vendor's product.

Customer Referral

Ask for customer referrals from each vendor. By checking with existing customers, you can find out more about the product. Ask the vendor's customers about how quickly and effectively the vendor responds to questions and problems with the product. Also ask how long it took them to implement the product and what they might do differently next time. Finally, ask how their last upgrade went and what they would most like to see improved in the product. Be aware that vendors are likely to give you the names of their most satisfied customers. However, every customer has experienced bumps with their products. So, be inquisitive.

Ask This

Ask for customer referrals from each vendor.

Vendor Health

You may also want to check the vendor's financials. The strength of your vendor's financial position and customer base helps ensure that the vendor will support your product well and will continue to evolve and improve with sufficient funding for product research and development.

Financial reports for public companies are readily available online. For private companies, you may find information by checking with Dun & Bradstreet. You may also want to check information from industry analysts on the financial health and market share of the products you are evaluating. Some well-regarded learning-technology industry analyst groups include Gartner Group, Forrester Research, Brandon Hall Research, and Bersin by Deloitte.

Request for Proposal

Once you've narrowed your group of finalists down, send a request for proposal to each of your finalists asking for pricing quotes, implementation timeframes, and support options. If you are considering a cloud solution, be sure to ask for hosting options, service guarantees, and pricing. For more information, see the section labeled "Product Costs" in Table 1-1.

Work with your purchasing or procurement departments when creating the RFP. They may have standard RFP templates and processes for you to follow, or they may assist directly in preparing and administering the RFP. Decide how long you want to allow for vendors to prepare their RFP responses. A reasonable period is two weeks. Compare the RFP responses, and don't be afraid to go back to each vendor to ask them for a better price or more feature options comparable to incentives the other vendor finalists are offering.

For clarity, the comparison chart in Table 6-6 explains the differences between an RFI, which you use in the product evaluation phase, and an RFP, which you use in the product selection phase.

Ask This

Ask for hosting options, service guarantees, and pricing if you are considering a cloud solution.

Table 6-6. Request for Information Versus Request for Proposal

Request for Information	Request for Proposal
• This lists all your LMS requirements along with two to six questions per requirement. • You ask a short list of vendors to respond to each question in the RFI. Responses should include thorough answers to all questions. Answers should describe how the vendor's product addresses your requirement. • While you may ask for general pricing information, getting a final price for your organization is usually not part of an RFI. • You and your colleagues review and score the responses to determine which products best meet your requirements These finalists are the potential candidates for the RFP.	• This lists all your requirements, along with the size of your learner audience, systems that need to be integrated with a new LMS, and whether you plan to migrate data from a legacy LMS. • You ask a few vendor finalists to submit a proposal to sell you their product. The quote should include licensing fees, hosting fees (for cloud solutions), maintenance and support fees, implementation costs, and the costs of any systems integrations, data migrations, product customizations, or other professional services needed to meet your requirements. • Of course, the price will likely be subject to negotiations with the vendor you select.

Foreman (2013b).

Step 5: Select a Product

The final step is to settle on a product. If possible, you can place your organization in a strong position to negotiate the best pricing and terms by selecting two or three finalist products, any of which will meet your needs. Don't be afraid to negotiate; remember that LMS vendors are eager to gain your business. To an LMS vendor, each new customer represents a multiyear revenue stream.

You have much more negotiating power when your evaluation results in more than one product finalist and you can reap the benefits of a vendor bidding war. But even if you have decided that a single vendor's product is the best fit for your organization, you can still negotiate for more than what the vendor has proposed. To gain your business, a vendor may offer you a discounted price, a free set of feature options that normally cost more, a better support package, a quicker start date for implementation, or other perks.

Always remember to build adequate time into your schedule to accommodate the contracting process. Contracting often involves the legal departments in both your organization and the vendor's and can sometimes take several weeks to complete. Once the contract is signed, you are ready to get busy with implementation.

Key Takeaways

This chapter described a proven process for analyzing your organization's learning management needs, defining requirements, and evaluating and selecting a product. The key takeaways are:

- A thorough needs analysis engages stakeholders and sponsors throughout your organization to identify your learning management system needs. Make sure to explore the viewpoints of your executive leadership, management, and IT.
- Clearly define and document your requirements and use them as the basis of your product selection criteria.
- Derive vetting criteria from your requirements; that is, distinctive requirements that will help you select a short list of vendors to evaluate.
- A funnel approach to your product evaluation activities helps you narrow hundreds of products down to the handful that are best matched to your requirements.
- Getting bids from two or three vendors whose products are equally good candidates for your organization positions you to negotiate the best terms and pricing.

The next three chapters explain how to implement your new LMS. Chapter 7 focuses on how to plan for your LMS implementation and configure your new product. Chapter 8 focuses on integrating your LMS with other systems and migrating your course content and learning-related data from your old LMS to the new one. Chapter 9 focuses on testing your LMS to make sure it is ready and going live.

CHAPTER 7

Planning Your Implementation and Configuring the LMS

The next three chapters cover how to implement your new LMS. This chapter applies mostly to corporate LMS and LCMS-LMS products. It explains how to assemble the right implementation team and plan your implementation. It goes into detail about the decisions you will need to make to configure your LMS so that it works best for your organization.

Your LMS evaluation and selection project is finally over. You have chosen an LMS that is well suited to your organization's needs and, because you involved your key stakeholders in the evaluation process, all parties have bought in to the selected LMS. Depending on negotiations and the due diligence of your legal department, the contract may have taken awhile to iron out, but everyone has signed on the dotted line and you're ready to begin a new project: LMS implementation.

LMS implementation usually involves a significant investment in cost and time, and represents a potential disruption to your organization. There are many moving parts, and as the old saying goes, "The devil is in the details." For a successful LMS implementation, you need significant planning and attention to detail. Allocating the right resources to accomplish each step in the process is critical. The alternative is a high risk of unwanted surprises, extensive delays, and problems likely to result in unhappy sponsors and end users.

In many organizations, L&D will need to collaborate with IT on LMS implementation. If this applies to you, it will be very important to build a rapport with your colleagues in IT. These professionals often use terminology that describes system and technical operations with which you may be unfamiliar. Your knowledge and understanding of this jargon will help build credibility, trust, and a good working relationship with IT as you evaluate, select, and implement your LMS. You can look up these terms in appendix B, "Glossary of IT Technical Jargon."

There are also some key terms that are frequently used by both L&D and IT, but with different definitions. As you work with IT on your LMS implementation, it will be important to distinguish the use of these terms to avoid misunderstanding. These dual-meaning terms can be found in appendix C, "Glossary of Terms With Different Meanings for L&D and IT."

Many organizations remember their last LMS implementation as a nightmare, but most of the problems they encountered could have been avoided. With the appropriate resources and planning and a lot of attention to detail, your new LMS can serve you well for many years to come.

How to Implement an LMS

LMS implementation typically involves six major steps: preparation and planning, configuration, systems integration, content and data migration, user acceptance testing, and go live (Figure 7-1). There are a few other key activities, such as communications and change management, that are not specific to LMS implementation, but must be part of any large-scale project for the highest likelihood of success. There are lots of books about communications planning and change management, so I won't cover them explicitly here.

This chapter covers the first two steps, planning and configuration. Chapter 8 covers steps three and four, integration and migration. And chapter 9 covers the final two steps, testing and go live.

Figure 7-1. The 6 Steps of LMS Implementation: Planning and Configuration

Step 1: Preparation and Planning

Careful preparation and planning is critical to the success of your LMS implementation. You must prepare by assembling an implementation team with the appropriate skill sets and freeing them from most of their other duties to allow sufficient time for them to work on the project.

Do not underestimate the amount of work involved in a large system implementation. I once worked with an organization that involved about a dozen people in the evaluation and selection process, and then left all the implementation details to a single person. This person was a dynamo. She relied heavily on the LMS vendor and external consultants, called for help from her colleagues at various stages, and worked many nights and weekends. But soon after the LMS went live, she was so exhausted and stressed that she resigned. It took the organization more than a year to recover from her loss and get the LMS initiative back on track. Spreading the workload across a team of people with the right combination of skills helps ensure the project's success throughout implementation and after going live.

With your team in place, you must develop a project plan to organize all your implementation steps, activities, and milestones. All team members must be involved so that their viewpoints and areas of expertise are represented in your project plan. Any steps you miss in your initial planning will surely emerge later in the implementation process. The earlier you identify and build them into your plan, the less likely they are to result in unanticipated costs and delays to your go live date.

Assemble Your Team

To get started, you must assemble your implementation team. Ideally, many of the people who were involved in the evaluation and selection process will continue to participate as you implement the LMS.

You need to assemble a core project team that is directly responsible for LMS implementation tasks and decision making. You also need an extended team that is activated at various points in the project, like testing the system before it goes live, when more people are required to handle the workload. Through their involvement in important implementation tasks, the extended team members will become acclimated to the LMS, gaining valuable hands-on experience with the system before it is fully up and running. An added benefit will be their enthusiastic support for the new LMS as you roll the system out.

Once you have identified and engaged your core team members, you are ready to get started. The extended team members can be identified later, after the core team has convened and you have begun to develop the project plan.

Core Team

The size of the core team is likely to reflect the size of your organization. In smaller organizations, two or three people may each wear several hats. Larger organizations may have a larger core team of five, six, or more people. But regardless of how many people are assigned, the core team should include at least six main roles:

1. The **team leader** is responsible for keeping the project on track and moving toward a successful outcome. A good team leader should be able to work effectively with all team members to remove obstacles, plan contingencies, interact with the LMS vendor, and escalate issues for resolution by upper management when necessary.
2. The **project manager** is responsible for keeping track of all the tasks, subtasks, resource assignments, dependencies, and due dates. An LMS implementation project has many moving parts, and a skilled project manager is critical to success.
3. An **e-learning technology specialist** is responsible for representing the organization's e-learning tools, platforms, and instructional models. Migrating e-learning courseware from a legacy system to a new LMS can be complex. The e-learning technology specialist will have primary responsibility for managing the web-based course migration and interoperability testing along with any native LMS content, such as surveys and assessments.
4. A **learning management system administrator** is responsible for representing the organization's administration needs, including security roles and permissions, course structures, competencies, credit types, certification, recertification, compliance, audiences and domains, user profiles and demographics, assignments and notifications, the course catalog and metadata, and reports. If you are unsure what

these learning management terms mean, you can find them explained for each of the three types of LMS products in chapters 2-4. The training administrator will play a key role in deciding how to configure the LMS to meet the organization's needs.

5. A **system usability specialist** is responsible for the look, feel, and ease of use of the system. This role is often filled by someone with a background in user interface design. The usability specialist is responsible for the logos, icons, branding, labels, style sheets, and color schemes that will be configured in the LMS, and may organize some usability tests to refine the system's ease of use before it goes live.
6. An **IT architect** is responsible for a range of system issues that may include security, single sign-on, data migration from the legacy LMS to the new LMS, and integration with other systems. If your organization is hosting the LMS on the premises—that is, in your own IT data center—then the IT architect may also be responsible for organizing the installation and maintenance of servers, network connectivity, and software.

In smaller organizations, the core team may comprise fewer people, and any two or three of these roles might be filled by a single person.

Extended Team

The extended team is activated at key points in the project. It comprises people who will work with the LMS frequently after implementation. Consider including e-learning authors, instructional designers, training and curriculum managers, administrators, and registrars. Be sure to involve stakeholders representing all content that will be delivered through the system, including HR learning and development, sales training, customer service center training, customer training, and other groups with training responsibilities. These extended team members will be involved in implementation activities like administrator training, content cleanup, systems integration testing, usability testing, and user acceptance testing. These activities will be described in chapters 8 and 9.

The extended team should also include IT production support, database administrators, systems integrators, network managers, and security officers. As extensions of the core team's IT architect role, these resources will be involved in systems-related tasks such as login and authentication, data migration, and systems integrations.

Implementation Timeframe

Assuming adequate resources are assigned, implementation of an LMS that is installed in your own data center for hosting on-premise can take anywhere from six to 12 months. Vendor-hosted solutions, often referred to as "cloud" or "software as a service (SaaS)" solutions, can take anywhere from three to nine months. Much of the time involved depends on how clearly your organization's requirements have been defined, how well suited your LMS is to those requirements, and the amount of variability and complexity that must be accommodated to support how your organization operates.

Failure to adequately define requirements can lead you to select a product that doesn't match your needs. I have seen more than one LMS implementation slowed by the organization's realization that the product does not do what they need it to do. Implementation time can double or more as you attempt to find creative workarounds, request custom enhancements, and change your existing processes to overcome system limitations. This leads to decreased support from key stakeholders, inflated implementation costs and schedules, and ultimately, a good deal of user dissatisfaction.

Project Plan

Planning is critical, not just at the outset of your project, but throughout. As the project proceeds, unanticipated needs and challenges will emerge, and your project plan will need to be continually expanded and refined. A strong project manager is a great asset to your LMS implementation.

The specifics of your plan will vary based on the needs of your organization. A good way to get started is to ask your LMS vendor to provide a project plan template. Any vendor-provided plan is likely to include all the tasks needed to implement the LMS from the *vendor's* point of view. You can start with the vendor's template and add the tasks that do not involve the vendor but are nevertheless important to your organization, like data cleanup, communications planning, change management planning, user acceptance testing, and end-user support.

Most project plans are likely to include higher-level categories of tasks such as LMS configuration, data transfer from the old LMS to the new one, systems integration development and testing, administrator training, report development, course catalog menu structure, and go-live planning. Each category will contain a collection of more specific tasks, some of which will need to happen sequentially and others in parallel. Depending on the specifics of your implementation, you may identify additional task categories to include in your plan.

Ask This

Ask your LMS vendor to provide a project plan template.

Step 2: Configuration

Most LMS products are designed to support a variety of ways in which organizations manage their learning programs. Because each organization is different, LMS products offer configurable parameters that you can set to reflect how your organization operates.

For example, one organization may want to use the LMS to train employees. The organization enters and updates its employees' names, position titles, organizations, contact information, and other profile data in a human resource management system. This organization wants to set up the HRMS to provide those data to the LMS. However, they don't want people changing their user profiles in the LMS, because that would put the two systems out of sync. As a result, they need to configure the LMS so that user profile data are updated automatically from the HRMS and cannot be changed by LMS users.

A different organization may want to use the LMS to train customers. It will need to configure the LMS to allow users to create and update their own accounts and user profile data.

To configure the LMS, your implementation team must select and enter your organization's preferred values for all the configurable features that control how the LMS works. Configuring an LMS can be complicated, with many decisions to make. Your team will need to think through the various options for each configurable parameter and reach agreement on how to set it up.

To complicate things further, your organization is likely to evolve in its use of the LMS over time, using more of the system's features, and adding more content and users. It is important that you make configuration decisions with the future learning management needs of your organization in mind. Some of the parameter values you configure can be changed easily at any time, while other changes may be more difficult. For these parameters, it is important to try to get it right the first time. The challenge is that you will be asked to make far-reaching configuration decisions, some of which may be difficult or impractical to change later on, without the benefit of hindsight and while you are still brand new to the system.

For example, let's say you've been using your new LMS for a year. You originally established three domains reflecting each of your business units. The users, content, administrators, course catalog, and branding of each domain are separate from those of the other business unit domains. This seemed like a good idea when you first implemented your LMS. At the time, you thought that each group had its own training needs. But over time you have discovered that there is actually a lot of overlap in the training needs of each group, and much of their content has been duplicated across domains. This has caused a significant amount of extra work for administrators, who need to publish the same course up to three times. Each business unit must schedule its own offerings of the same course, making it difficult to optimize class sizes with attendees from all units.

So you've decided to collapse the three domains down to a single one. Unfortunately, this will not be easy. You must move all the content, users, and data to a single domain; consolidate your administrators and rework their roles and permissions; change some of the programming in your HRMS data integration; test the system to make sure you didn't miss any details or lose any data; and communicate the change to users. It's almost like implementing a new LMS.

You may think your LMS vendor will provide you with guidance and consulting so that you avoid making costly configuration mistakes. Well, LMS vendors are foremost in the business of selling their product to as many organizations as possible. Your LMS vendor will train you on how the product works and then expect you to make system configuration decisions based on what you have learned about the product and your knowledge of your organization. While most vendors will do their best to advise you on your options, your vendor cannot reasonably learn the ins and outs of each of its customer's organizations to provide the necessary customer advocacy, consulting, and guidance. Your vendor's expertise with its product and your core team's expert knowledge of your organization's needs must meet somewhere in the middle. Many organizations engage a third-party implementation consultant to learn the details of how the organization manages learning, advocate for its needs, advise on its LMS configuration decisions, and help ensure the success of the project.

The configuration decisions you will need to make involve understanding your data and operations, and understanding the data fields, functionality, and capabilities of your new LMS. Configuration decision making can take two to four weeks or more depending on the complexity of the system, the scope of your requirements, and the availability of your decision makers. Following are some of the most important parameters you will need to configure.

Unique ID, Username, and Password

Each user in the LMS must have a unique ID. Depending on the nature of your organization and who is using your LMS, you may decide to use an employee ID that is generated by the HRMS, a student ID that is generated by the student information system, or a member ID that is generated by a professional association's member management system. For organizations that are not synchronizing the user accounts with a source system, the LMS may automatically generate a unique ID for each new user account. Some organizations use the username entered by a new user when they create their account as the unique ID. Like on many popular retail websites, this may be an email address or some other form of unique identification.

The username and password allow users to log in to the system. Each user must enter a username and password, which, when matched with a unique ID, authenticates the user and provides access to the system. In many configurations, users can change their username and password or retrieve lost credentials any time. However, in configurations that involve single sign-on, a separate system usually controls the username and password, and users can't change them in the LMS.

User Profiles

You will need to decide what user demographic data you will need, where it is currently stored and managed, and where to put it in the LMS. The demographic data you collect in your LMS may differ depending on the nature of your organization. For example, in a business setting, LMS demographic data may include the user's name and contact information; job function and organization; manager; employment status, such as part time or full time; time in current job; time in current organization; and hire date. In a K-12 or higher education setting, LMS demographic data may include name and contact information, grade level or year, degree program, and major. In a professional association setting, LMS demographic data may include name and contact information, company, membership status, and the year that membership was established.

When deciding how to configure the user profile, consider what data are needed for your LMS reports and how you want to segment the users in your system. For example, you may want to determine which courses are in highest demand by people in a specific job role, functional area, business unit, or region. You may want to take a look at pass-fail rates for students in a specific degree program, major, and academic year. You may need to assign new hire orientation training to people based on their hire date, job role, and region. Keep in mind that user profile information can also be used to provide personalized views of the content in your LMS, as explained in the section "Domains and Audiences."

Organization Hierarchies

Many LMS products support organizational hierarchies that can be configured to match your organization's structure. Think about your company's org chart; the LMS would have an organization node associated with each box on the chart. People are then associated with the department or group in which they work, within the organizational hierarchy. This approach allows you to deploy courses that may be customized to a specific department or collection of departments. You can run reports for the entire enterprise, one specific department, or a department and all the departments below it. The organization hierarchy in an LMS is often imported from an HRMS.

In an extended enterprise solution where the LMS is also being used to train business partners, such as distributors, dealers, and suppliers, the organization structure may be configured to reflect the companies with which the organization does business. For organizations that sell training programs directly to the public, customers may be associated with a single customer node or one of several market segments or product groups. If your company sells products or services business to business, then customers may be organized into company accounts or industries. In Figure 7-2, you can see how the LMS organization structure reflects the way the company is organized.

Domains and Audiences

Some LMS products allow you to configure multiple domains, sometimes called multitenancy. This approach is particularly useful for extended enterprise solutions, where you need to train employees, suppliers, distributers, and customers. Without domains, it is difficult to prevent customers from accessing content designed for employees only. Domains allow you to place employee user accounts, internal courses, and administrators in the employee domain and customers, customer training courses, and another set of administrators in the customer domain. Each domain can be distinctly branded and configured, giving each group of users its own look, feel, and feature set. You can enable e-commerce in the customer domain, disable it in the employee domain, and run separate reports for each domain. The result is like having multiple LMS installations for the price of one. In Figure 7-3, you can see the organization structure of an LMS that has two domains, one for customers and another for employees.

Figure 7-2. Example of an LMS Organization Structure

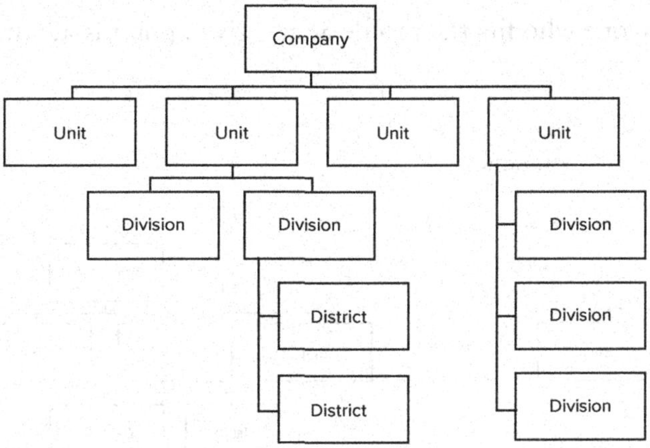

It is important to note that some changes to your domain structure may be difficult to make after the product is up and running. For example, it may be relatively easy to add a new domain, but removing or reorganizing existing domains that already contain users and content can be very complex, so keep it as simple as you can.

Guidelines for Planning Your Domains

- Keep it simple. Use as few domains as possible. A single domain is often enough.
- Be sure you have a clear need for multiple domains. Consider what is unique in terms of the content, administration, branding, reports, and features needed by the users in each domain.
- Only configure what you need today. If you set up domains for possible future use, you will probably get it wrong.

Many LMS systems enable you to configure audiences based on user profile information. For example, you may define an audience comprising people in the northeast region who work in sales, or people whose hire date was within the last three months. Audiences enable you to assign training to groups of users in a way that is self-organizing. Without audiences, you would need to assign training to a list of named users, which means that you would need to update the list whenever someone changes jobs or leaves the company. When you configure an audience based on profile information, anyone who fits the profile at any given point is automatically included in the audience.

Figure 7-3. Example of Two LMS Domains

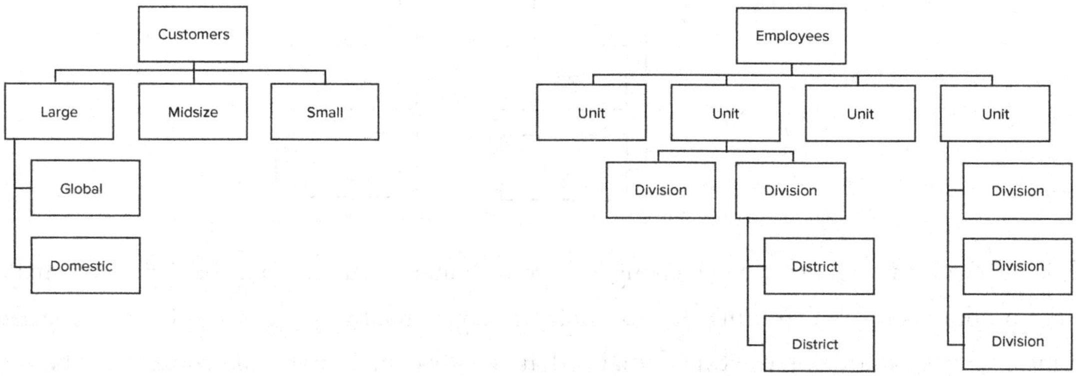

You can restrict a course's visibility to people within each audience. For example, someone in sales may see a different set of course offerings from someone in IT, finance, or manufacturing. This approach makes the LMS easier to use by providing users with shorter and more relevant course lists. It also avoids the risk of people mistakenly registering and showing up for the wrong course.

Administrator Security Roles

Each security role you configure in your system represents a type of LMS administrator. For example, your implementation may require an instructor role, a course developer role, a course scheduler role, a registrar, and a super-user who can change the LMS configuration. To accomplish this, you would establish five security roles. You can then set the specific permissions for each role. In most LMS products, permissions can be set at a granular level. So, for example, an instructor may be able to view a roster, take attendance, and mark people complete, but may not be able to publish new courses to the system. A course developer may be able to create new course structures and create and publish courses, but may not be able to change the organizational hierarchy or user profile configuration. During the LMS configuration process, you will define the security roles your organization will use and the specific permissions for each role. Once user accounts are loaded into the system, you can associate users with each role.

Some LMS products enable a single user to have multiple roles. Other systems allow only one role per user. If your LMS supports multiple domains, a user may be able to be assigned different roles in each domain. You will need to design your security roles in a way that matches how your LMS works.

Course Catalog

An LMS course catalog is a comprehensive list of the courses you offer. People can browse the catalog to find the courses they want.

In some LMS products, the catalog is menu driven. People navigate through the catalog's menus and submenus until they reach a list of relevant courses. In other LMS products, the catalog is a single list of all courses. People filter the list by selecting a topic, delivery method, and other parameters to narrow the selection to the courses most relevant to their needs.

You will need to design your catalog structure, and later set up your courses so that they appear in the right place in the catalog. When you configure your course catalog, you will need to think about clarity and balance.

Metadata

Course metadata consist of a set of properties or tags that describe your courses. For example, you may decide to configure a metadata property labeled *delivery mode.* The values for this property may be labeled *web-based training (self-paced), live webinar, recorded webinar,* and *classroom.* You may decide to configure another property that indicates the language in which the course is offered. Every time someone publishes a course in the LMS, the publisher selects a value for each metadata property.

Guidelines for Creating Your Course Catalog

- Avoid ambiguity. A vague menu item is not helpful. Menu items labeled *skills and knowledge, miscellaneous,* or *other* do not provide a clear indication of what courses will be found under them.
- Make each menu item distinct. For example, menu items labeled *soft skills, interpersonal skills,* and *sales skills* are not sufficiently distinct from one another.
- Make sure items in the same menu are categorically similar. For example, menu items that represent subjects, like *time management, working with teams,* and *communications skills,* should not be mixed with menu items that do not represent subjects, like *new courses* or *courses in Spanish.*
- Menu-item labels should be succinct and should not require additional explanation.
- Design the catalog so that the courses are evenly distributed among the menu items. Let's say your catalog has one menu item labeled *products and services* containing 70 courses, another labeled *submitting vouchers* containing three courses, and a third menu item labeled *policies and procedures* containing nine courses. Consider deleting the *submitting vouchers* menu item and moving those courses into *policies and procedures.* Consider dividing the course-heavy *products and services* menu item into five or six menu items representing different product families or types of services. This will result in a more balanced course catalog, which is easier for users to navigate.
- If you have dozens of courses, try using a flat menu. If you have hundreds of courses, consider using submenus.
- Avoid creating menu items that result in a mix of courses and more submenu items. If you are using submenus, attach the courses to the submenu items rather than items in the main menu. This will result in a more predictable catalog, where all items at a given menu level behave the same way.
- Make sure there are no "orphaned" menu items. These are dead-ended menu items that, when clicked, produce no courses at all.

In some systems, you can configure each metadata property as either a required or optional field. For example, if you set *language* as a required field, administrators will not be able to save or publish a course without first setting a language value.

Some systems allow you to configure a metadata property so that multiple values can be associated with a single course. For example, an instructor-led course may have a delivery mode value of *classroom*, while a blended course may be associated with multiple delivery modes such as *webinar, self-paced, assignment, test,* and *survey.*

Metadata properties usually appear on the course details page, which is displayed after a course title has been selected from the catalog or search results. Along with the course title and description, metadata provide essential information to help people decide how to spend their valuable training time.

Course and Curriculum Structures

A course may include multiple learning activities, such as a reading assignment, a pretest, a self-paced module, attendance in a classroom or webinar session, a mastery test, and a survey. These activities may need to be configured to be taken either in any order or in an enforced sequence. Some activities may be mandatory, others optional. The course's structure depends on which learning activities are used and in what order. In Figure 7-4, you can see an example of three standardized course structures: an instructor-led course followed by an online assessment, a live webinar followed by a survey, and a SCORM course followed by a survey.

Figure 7-4. LMS Course Structures Example

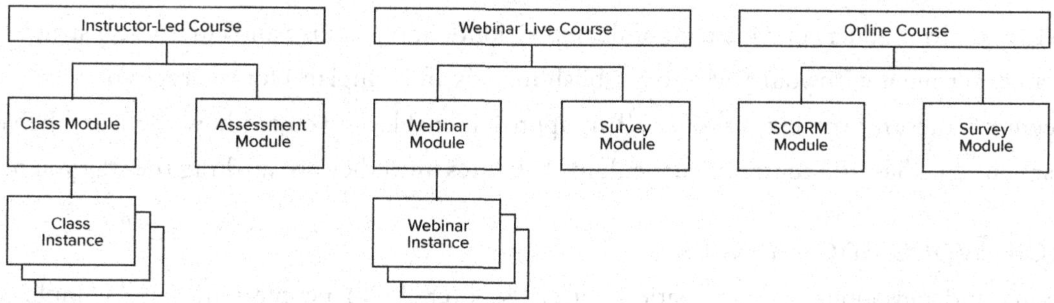

A curriculum may include a number of courses that may or may not need to be taken in sequence. Again, some may be mandatory and others optional. The criteria for earning completion credit may vary from curriculum to curriculum. So, courses have structures, and curricula have structures, or meta-structures. Figure 7-5 illustrates a curriculum structure where the learner must complete courses A, B, and C in sequence, then complete either course D or course E, and finally complete course F.

Figure 7-5. LMS Curriculum Structure Example

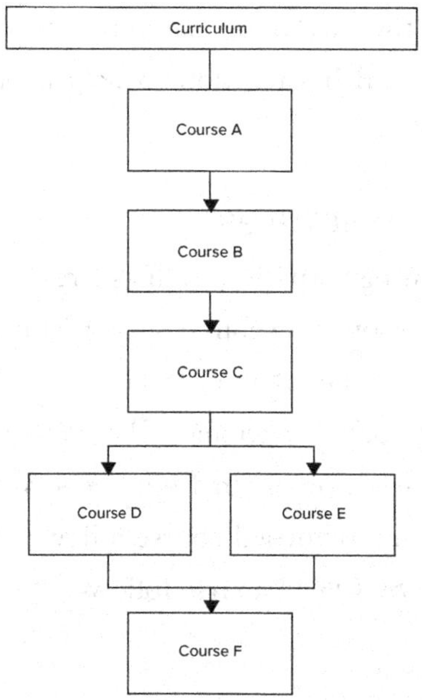

Many LMS products provide a lot of flexibility for defining course and curriculum structures. You can experiment with your LMS to establish models and templates for the types of course and curriculum structures you expect to use. This approach enables to you see how the LMS behaves so that you can adjust the course or curriculum structures until they are working the way you need.

Credit Types and Credits

Learning and development organizations often issue credit to people who have completed a course. Most LMS products allow you to configure any number of credit types. For example, one credit type may be labeled *credit hours,* while another is labeled *continuing education units.*

When someone publishes a course in the system, they may select one or more of the available credit types and enter the number of credits for each type to award people upon course completion. People who complete the course are automatically awarded the credits, which appear in their transcript and on the course completion certificate.

Many systems allow you to run reports by credit type. This can be useful in regulatory compliance or accreditation reporting.

Evaluations and Assessments

Many LMS products have built-in evaluation (survey) and assessment (test) tools. The advantage to using a native LMS tool is that you can easily view reports at the question level, which enables you to perform item analysis and determine the validity of your survey or test. The disadvantage is that if you switch LMS products, you may need to redevelop the assessment. You may also find it difficult to migrate the evaluation and assessment results contained in the old LMS, especially if the two systems' features differ. These disadvantages are especially pertinent to corporate LMS products. Academic LMS products that support the IMS Global® Question & Test Interoperability® specification provide easier methods to transfer tests and test results from one system to another. Chapter 5 has more information about this specification and others.

If you decide to use a survey tool that's built into your LMS to deliver a course completion survey, you'll need to configure the survey and enter the questions and Likert scale anchors.

Sometimes, LMS products have unexpected constraints when it comes to survey reporting. Ask your vendor to explain how you can configure a standard survey for use in all courses and run survey results reports in all the ways you need to view data. For example, you may want to see the results for everyone who has taken a specific course or group of courses over the last year, or all the people who took a specific class, or all the people who have taken any course taught by a specific instructor.

If you can't get the reports you need from your LMS, you may be better off using a third-party survey tool. In that case, you'll need to devise a way to identify each survey with a course, class, and instructor in your LMS. If you decide to use a third-party testing or surveying tool, you will need to explore how the tool interoperates with the LMS. You may be able to use the ADL SCORM standard or simply serve up the test or survey in the third-party system after launching it from the LMS. Check with your survey tool vendor and LMS vendor to discuss options.

Ask This

Ask your vendor to explain how you can configure a standard survey for use in all courses and run survey results reports in all the ways you need to view data.

Competencies

Some organizations are interested in implementing a competency model in their LMS. Typically, an LMS will allow you to create a list of competencies and a proficiency scale that can be applied to any competency. For example, a user may have novice proficiency in one competency and expert proficiency in another.

In many LMS products, competencies can be used to direct people to training. To do this, competencies are associated with jobs, people, assessments, and courses. A job requires a certain set of competencies, each at a specific level of proficiency. A course covers a set of competencies. A person can take a self-assessment to compare their current proficiency level for each competency with the level their job role requires. Their competency gaps are identified in the assessment results. They can then search for courses that address those competencies. As you can see in Figure 7-6, competency-based assessments can be used to connect people, jobs, and courses in an LMS.

In talent management systems, competencies can be used in even more ways, including recruiting, selection, and career development. Job descriptions may reflect the competencies required for the job. Applicants may be assessed based on the competencies they describe in resumes or articulate in interviews. Employees may use competency-based self-assessments to compare their current skills with those required for a desired job role, and then use the reported gaps to create a professional development plan.

Configuring competencies in your LMS can be a big job. First, you will need to load all your competencies and your proficiency scale into the LMS. If you have different competencies for different job functions, all the competencies will need to be added and associated with the relevant jobs. If you decide to create competency-based assessments, you will need to design the assessment questions and scoring methods.

Figure 7-6. How Competencies Are Used in an LMS

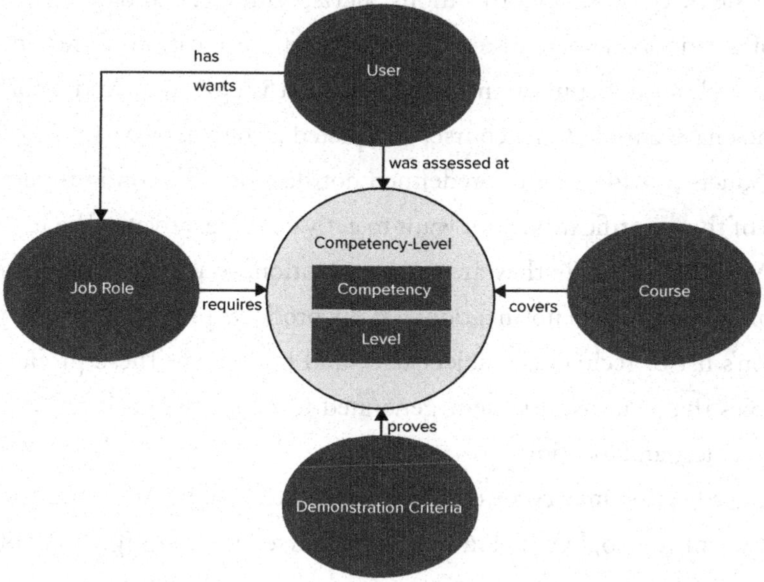

Finally, you will need to associate relevant competencies with courses. You can do that by simply associating one or more competencies directly with a course, without considering proficiency levels, or you can associate each relevant competency at one or more specific proficiency levels with a course. Think about how you want your competency-course relationships to work, and check with your LMS vendor to determine what approaches the product supports.

> **Ask This**
>
> Think about how you want your competency-course relationships to work, and check with your LMS vendor to determine what approaches the product supports.

Notifications

LMS products provide three types of notifications: alerts, reminders, and confirmations. An alert may notify users of a canceled course or a change to a date or location. A reminder may notify users of a class that is about to begin or an assignment that is past due. And a confirmation may notify users that they have enrolled in a course, completed a course, or passed a test.

Most LMS products provide a set of predefined notifications. To configure notifications, you must decide which of these notifications you want to activate or deactivate. The more email people receive from an LMS, the less likely they are to pay attention, so to avoid spamming users, it is a good idea to turn off all unessential notifications. Many products provide a way for you to customize each notification's list of recipients, subject text, and body text. These products provide you with a set of variables that can insert system-generated text into the notification, such as course title, student name, dates, and location.

For example, a notification may come out of the box with a registration confirmation message that is automatically sent to people who enrolled in a course. The message body may contain the following text and variables.

> <First name>,
> You have successfully registered in <course name> at <location> from <start date> to <end date>.
> The Learning and Development Organization

A very important note of caution: Disable the LMS email send capability before you go live. You don't want to send unintended email notifications to people while you are migrating data or configuring and testing the system. This may involve working with your vendor to ensure that the LMS email send capability is disabled in some other way.

Reports

An LMS provides a set of out-of-the-box reports. Many products also include reporting tools that enable you to configure your own custom reports. Some even provide advanced capabilities for creating graphical reports and dashboards.

Many products allow you to export your reports to Excel or CSV, PDF, and sometimes XML. Exporting to Excel or CSV, which can be opened in Excel, is especially useful if you want to adjust the data and layout, sort and filter it in a variety of ways, or generate graphs and charts. PDF can be useful if you need to distribute the report in a printable format. XML is a good format if you need to import the data into another system or application.

Early in the implementation process, you need to identify and list all the reports your organization needs. The data in your reports will guide many of your LMS configuration and data migration decisions. Be sure to identify who needs the report, how often, and why. As you consider why a report is needed, think about what decisions will be made or what actions will be taken from the report results. If the report's purpose cannot be clearly articulated, then it will probably not be used in the long run. In my experience, out of the hundreds of potential reports available in some LMS products, many organizations tend to use only a handful.

Defining Your LMS Report Needs

1. Document who needs the report, how often, and why.
2. Make a list of all data to be included in the report.
3. Create a mock-up of how the data should appear in the report. You may need different layouts for an HTML version of the report and an Excel version.
4. Report filters allow you to limit the amount of data in the report. Define how you will need to filter the report, such as by enrollment date range, completion date range, course or course group, or user or user group.
5. Sorting allows you to order the data in the HTML version of the report (the Excel version has its own sort features). Decide which columns you want to use to sort the data, and in which direction. In some LMS products, clicking on any column header in an HTML report will sort the data alphanumerically or by date, and may even toggle the data in forward (A to Z) or reverse (Z to A) alphabetical order.

You may need to configure security and roles and permissions that control who can see a given report. Some LMS products let you schedule a process that automatically runs a report and emails a link to a recipient list. To see the report, these people must have user accounts in the LMS.

Some products allow you to send the report as an Excel or PDF attachment in the email message to a list of email recipients who may not have user accounts in the LMS. Consider how you need to distribute your reports, and make sure your LMS can be configured to support your approach.

E-Commerce

If you need to charge individuals for taking your courses, you will need an LMS with e-commerce features. These systems typically allow people to select courses from the catalog and place them in a shopping cart. Upon checkout, the person pays for the course or courses in the shopping cart, which completes the enrollment process. Payment can be done with a credit card or online payment service such as PayPal. To accept and process these payments, you will need to contract with a third-party payment processing service.

To configure e-commerce, you'll need to enter information about your payment processing service provider. You must enter the price for each course that requires payment, so you'll also need to configure the currency type you're using in the LMS. Some LMS products that support domains allow different currency type and payment processing services to be configured in each domain.

Branding, Layout, and Welcome Page

Most LMS products provide a way for you to upload your organization's logo and configure your preferred color scheme. You can then customize your own homepage with images, text, video, audio, links, and anything else you can do in HTML. Many products provide WYSIWIG (what you see is what you get) controls so that you can work on your homepage content and layout without needing to be an HTML expert.

Some LMS products provide advanced options to further customize the look and feel throughout the system. These systems may provide access to the cascading style sheets (CSS), which are used to control global and page-specific fonts, font sizes, font styles, font colors, background colors, paragraph spacing, buttons and numbering, and hyperlink colors. However, changing these CSS settings requires advanced HTML and CSS skills. Changing a font size can affect the system's page layouts when viewed in a browser or mobile device. Take care to check the results of your CSS changes in all LMS pages.

By establishing a set of design standards, you provide a more consistent look to the LMS pages and make them fit in with other websites in your organization.

LMS configuration requires a lot of attention to detail. Once it is done, the system will begin to look and feel more familiar, like it belongs to your organization. Be sure to involve the right people in the decision-making process. You will need to take a thoughtful approach to group planning and decision making, considering not only your current needs, but also your future needs. Your LMS configuration decisions will determine how well the LMS is aligned with how your organization operates. The right configuration will save your administrators time and effort and provide a satisfying user experience.

Key Takeaways

This chapter focused on how to assemble your LMS implementation team, what to expect in terms of the implementation timeframe, and the first two steps of the implementation process: planning and making LMS configuration decisions. The key takeaways are:

- A core team will have primary responsibility for the success of the implementation, and an extended team will be involved in several of the more resource-intensive implementation tasks, like user acceptance testing.
- Implementation of an LMS hosted on-premise can take six to 12 months. Implementation of an LMS in the cloud can take three to nine months. If your requirements were not well defined and your system is not well suited to your organization's needs, the implementation is likely to take much longer.
- Planning is rigorous at the beginning of the implementation process and continues all the way up to the day on which your system goes live. A strong project manager is a key asset to your core team.
- There are many configuration decisions to be made as you implement your LMS related to things like user authentication, user profiles, organizational structure, domains and audiences, security roles and permissions, course catalog, metadata, courses and curriculum structures, credit types, evaluations and assessments, competencies, notifications, reports, e-commerce, and branding and homepage layout.

The next chapter covers systems integration and how to move all your data and content from a legacy system to your new LMS.

CHAPTER 8

Integrating Your LMS With Other Systems and Migrating Legacy Data

This chapter applies to all three types of LMS products. It describes the systems that many organizations integrate with the LMS. It also explains the steps and considerations for moving your courses and user data from an old LMS to a new one.

As discussed in the last chapter, LMS implementation typically involves six major steps. This chapter covers steps three and four, integration and migration.

Figure 8-1. The 6 Steps of LMS Implementation: Integration and Migration

Integration is required when two applications must continually share the same data. Migration happens when data must be moved out of an old system that will be retired and into the new

system that will replace it. You will need to work with your IT department on these steps. If you don't have an IT department, ask your vendors to help with integration and migration. Typically, your LMS vendor will provide professional services to help you manage these two steps. You can also engage the vendor of any systems to be integrated with the LMS and, for migration, the vendor of the old LMS you are replacing.

While some organizations deploy an LMS without integrating with any other systems, most need to fit the LMS into their broader IT technology infrastructure. This may involve integration with HR systems, single sign-on solutions, portals, enterprise search tools, financial systems, data warehouses, and other applications.

Ask This

Ask your vendors to help with integration and migration if you don't have an IT department.

Migrating your existing courseware and data to an LMS can be one of the most complex aspects of implementation. If this is your organization's first LMS, you may need to migrate data from a homegrown system, spreadsheets, or a lightweight database. If you are moving from one system to another, you'll need to get the data out of the old system and into the new one.

No two LMS products are exactly alike; each product has its own data structure. Your new system may require fields that are optional or completely missing from your old one. Your new LMS may allow up to 1,024 characters in the course description field, while your old one was restricted to 512 characters. Your new LMS may keep track of the user's course registration date, while the old one only kept track of the completion date. These differences complicate the data migration process.

Step 3: Systems Integration

Systems integrations streamline the user experience and improve data integrity by synchronizing data between systems. Let's say you have two separate systems that serve the same set of users. Both systems have user accounts and user profiles. Without integration, every user must create a separate user account, populate a separate user profile, and log in to each system separately. If users are not careful about maintaining the exact same information in their accounts and profiles in both systems, the data in the two systems will not match. When the data in two systems are duplicated and do not match, it is difficult or impossible to determine which system has the correct data.

If these two systems were integrated, a user would simply create an account and profile in one system. The data from that system would automatically be synchronized with the second system. A user would only need to log in to one to be granted access to both systems.

There are a number of systems with which an LMS may be integrated. This chapter describes some of the most common systems integrations, many of which you are likely to encounter.

Your core team member from IT will probably take the lead on any integration projects. The amount of time needed to complete an integration project varies based on the complexity of the integration and the availability of resources to specify, design, develop, and test the integration solution.

Systems That Manage User Accounts and Profiles

One of the most common LMS systems integrations is with another system that contains user accounts and profile information. For an academic organization, this is a student information system, which contains information about each student's degree program, major area of study, coursework, grades and grade point average, academic year, contact, financial status, and demographics. For a professional association, this is a member management system or associate management system, which contains information about each member's professional role, professional certifications, contact, membership status, and demographics. For a company, this is a human resource management system or human resource information system, which contains information about each employee's job role, organization, region, hire date, and level. Some businesses use their LMS for training the "extended enterprise," which may include some combination of customers, suppliers, dealers, agents, and distributers. These organizations have some sort of identity management solution in place to keep track of their extended enterprise users. If your organization has one of these systems, you will probably want to develop a system interface to synchronize user accounts with the LMS.

It does not make sense to manage the same data separately in two different systems. Because these user accounts and profiles originate in another system, you can avoid countless hours of duplicated effort and costly mistakes by simply importing the data from the originating system, rather than re-creating it manually in the LMS.

You can import the user accounts before going live with your LMS so that you can test the various features and functionality of the system. But what happens when new people are added to the organization, others leave, and user profiles change? Your LMS needs to remain synchronized with the originating system. This happens using recurring data feeds, which can be automated so that no human intervention is required. They can be scheduled to occur during off-peak hours, typically nights and weekends. If your organization operates in multiple time zones, check with your IT organization. They will have knowledge of your organization's network traffic and will be able to recommend the best time for data feeds to be scheduled.

LMS products provide mechanisms to import recurring data feeds from these systems. Your IT group will need to develop a program to extract the data from the user account system and format it according to your LMS vendor's specifications so that it can be imported into the LMS. The entire process can be scheduled to run automatically on a nightly basis. Your IT group may refer to this as a nightly feed or extract-transform-load (ETL) process.

Ask This

If your organization operates in multiple time zones, ask your IT organization about the best time for data feeds to be scheduled.

If your organization does not have a system where user accounts are originated, you will need to configure the LMS to create and manage user accounts. This is often the case in many government agency LMS implementations.

If you have a limited number of users, you may want to implement an account creation or change request process outside the LMS and restrict LMS account creation and management to administrators. This will ensure that only authorized users can access the LMS and decrease the risk of user-generated errors. For example, a community college instructor might create accounts for the continuing adult education students participating in a semester-long class.

If you have too many users to manage accounts administratively, you can configure the system to allow users to create their own accounts. Be aware that this approach is more likely to result in duplicate accounts, incomplete user profiles, and other inaccurate user data. One approach to remedy this is to find an LMS that requires users to enter a unique email address when creating a new account. The system then emails the user and waits for a response before validating the account. This approach is used by many public websites where users can create their own accounts.

Whatever approach you take to managing user accounts, be sure to check your license agreement with the LMS vendor to ensure that you are licensed for the number of users who have accounts in your system.

Ask This

Check your license agreement with the LMS vendor to ensure that you are licensed for the number of users who have accounts in your system.

Single Sign-On

Another frequent LMS integration is with a single sign-on solution. To avoid requiring end users to log in to different systems with different logins, some organizations have implemented single sign-on, which enables a user to log in to the network once and gain access to multiple applications through a silent authentication process that accepts credentials from the SSO solution and circumvents the login page of those systems.

Each LMS product may support its own selection of commonly used SSO methods. You may hear your vendor spew head-spinning technical terms like *SAML (security assertion markup language), oAuth (open authorization), Microsoft ADFS (Active Directory Federation Services),* or *Kerberos.* Put your IT department in touch with your LMS vendor directly to determine how they can best integrate the LMS with your organization's SSO solution.

An important factor your IT organization must be aware of while planning LMS SSO implementation is the handling of deep links, which may be embedded in system-generated email notifications. A deep link is a web address to a specific page in the LMS, such as a course details page or a user profile page. Usually, people must already be logged in to the LMS to view these pages. So, clicking on the deep link in an email message when you are not already logged in to the LMS may result in an error message like "page not found" or "you are not authorized to view this page," or even more confusingly, it may drop you off at the LMS homepage. The deep link problem is not limited to email messages. You may also need to place a deep link on your company's portal or another website, to function as a shortcut to a specific page within the LMS.

Ask This

Put your IT department in touch with your LMS vendor directly to determine how they can best integrate the LMS with your organization's SSO solution.

The best way to handle a deep link is to ensure that the SSO solution checks whether the user is already authenticated and, if not, redirects the user to the login page. It should then redirect the user to the original deep link. If, after a user logs in, the LMS finds that the user's profile has some required fields that have not been populated, it may redirect them to the profile page(s) to enter values into those fields. During the entire transaction, the SSO must hold onto the deep link URL so that the user can be sent there after authentication is completed.

Portal

In some cases, it makes sense to pull data from the LMS and display it on your portal. The data may be general, such as a list of courses, or personalized, such as a transcript. I have worked with companies that have advertised courses by placing them in noticeable places on the portal, and with professional associations that have advertised their certification programs with a general description and link to each course in the program.

Many LMS products offer two methods for integration with a portal. One of these methods is to capture the web address of a specific course in your LMS and paste it into a portal page as a deep link. When users click on the link on the portal page, it takes them directly to the course details page in the LMS. This approach must be maintained manually. For example, if you deactivate a course in the LMS, you must be sure to remove any corresponding deep link from your portal pages.

Another method, called an application programming interface (API), allows your IT department to access the data and functionality of your LMS programmatically. Your IT group can write a program that uses the LMS API to pull data from your LMS and post it in the portal. This approach can be fully automated so that no human intervention is required, and, if designed and developed properly, it ensures that the LMS data shown in the portal are always accurate.

Ask your LMS vendor to provide documentation on how to use its API and provide it to your IT department. Explain to IT what you are trying to accomplish through your portal integration and ask them to evaluate the LMS API to determine whether it can be done. You may want to provide some mock-ups illustrating your vision for what the portal pages will look like once the integration is complete. Mock-ups will help your IT department plan and implement the solution as you intend.

Ask This

Ask your LMS vendor to provide documentation on how to use its API and provide it to your IT department.

Enterprise Search

A 2013 study I conducted with the eLearning Guild showed that one of the three most important LMS features to respondents was search (Foreman 2013). The same survey showed that search also happened to be one of the three features respondents were unhappy with in their current LMS.

Many large organizations have deployed an enterprise search platform to find content stored in multiple systems. In this case, an employee can search on a topic and view results from the company's portal, knowledge bases, document management systems, and social networking sites. For example, let's say an employee who wants information on how the company handles quality assurance (QA) for the products it manufactures searches "quality assurance." A list of items is returned, including a hyperlink to the employee portal page about the organization's QA policies, a collection of knowledge base articles explaining quality processes and giving examples of how they are applied, several documents containing specific quality process steps and procedures, and hyperlinks to contact information in an employee directory for QA specialists who can answer questions on the topic.

In the past, LMS content has rarely been included in enterprise search results. In recent years, some organizations have integrated their enterprise search platform with the LMS so that courses are included in the search results along with documents, posts, and articles from other repositories. In the QA example, search results would also contain courses on quality assurance.

There are two main methods for integration: federated search and aggregated search.

A federated search solution allows a user to enter a search string into the enterprise search box, which in turn triggers multiple concurrent searches using the native search features in each content repository. Figure 8-2 illustrates how a federated search works.

Figure 8-2. How a Federated Search Works

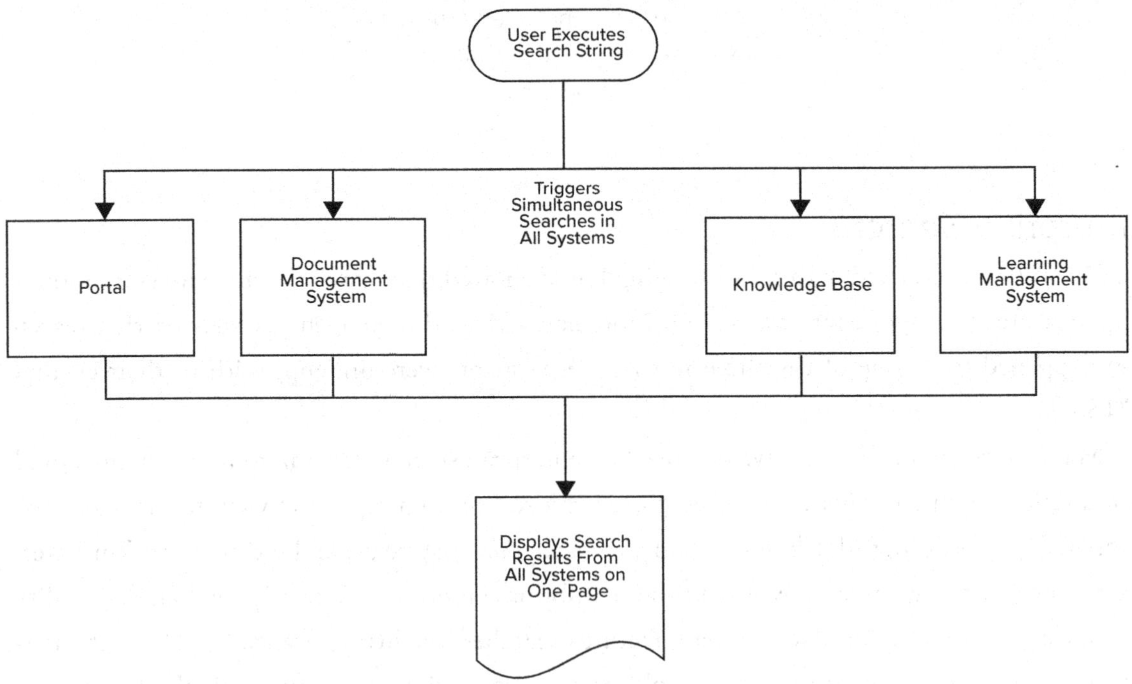

The key benefit of this approach is that a user can enter a search string in one place and get results that include LMS courses along with information and documents from a document management, knowledge management, or content management system.

An aggregated search solution "crawls" each repository periodically, creating a centralized, master index of the content. The user's search string is compared with the master index, and results are displayed with links to their locations in each of the repositories. Figure 8-3 illustrates how an aggregated search works.

Figure 8-3. How an Aggregated Search Works

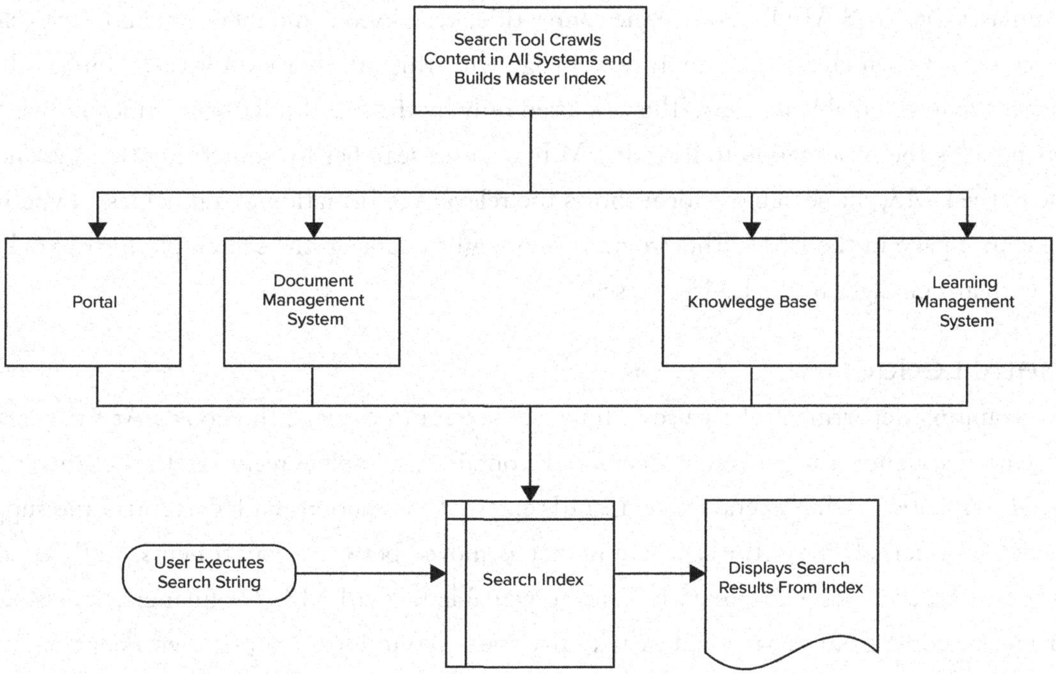

This approach has the same benefit as the federated system, as well as the added benefit of a superior search tool. Most enterprise search platforms operate similarly to the web searches to which people have become accustomed. These tools offer advanced search features such as proximity ranking (most to least relevant), controlled vocabulary (synonyms and acronyms), all forms of a word, and spelling correction ("did you mean . . ."). The challenge lies in getting the search platform to crawl the LMS database and index its course titles, descriptions, and metadata in a way that makes it searchable. This can involve some programming time and effort from your IT department, and the results depend on the quality of the LMS data. When done well, this type of search is far superior to the search feature offered by most LMS products, where an incorrect spelling, alternative word form, or mismatched capitalization can exclude relevant content from the search results.

Integrating your LMS with a federated search platform is often accomplished through some programming that uses the search platform's API to trigger an LMS search using the LMS API.

Integrating your LMS with an aggregated search platform is often done through development of a custom software program that runs on a scheduled, recurring basis, such as nightly. The program uses the LMS API to retrieve the course title, description, and metadata and a hyperlink to the course. It then creates a temporary webpage with this information for each course. These webpages are not available to users. They are used only by the search platform, which crawls the pages and adds the information to its index. When a user searches for something that matches a course in the LMS, the search platform shows the relevant information and provides a hyperlink to the course page in the LMS. The program runs nightly to keep the search platform synchronized with any changes to the LMS courses.

General Ledger

Your accounting department likely uses a financial system to manage the books. At the heart of this financial system is the general ledger, which contains a complete record of the organization's financial transactions. The general ledger records external transactions with customers and suppliers as well as internal transactions, where money is moved between departments. Let's say that department A purchases a course and makes it available in the LMS. No financial transactions occur when people from department A take the course. But when people from departments B and C take the course, their departments must reimburse department A. This interdepartmental billing is managed in the general ledger.

If your organization manages interdepartmental billing for courses that are licensed by one organization and taken by people in other organizations, then you may want to consider automating the process by integrating your LMS with your general ledger.

The first step is to ensure that the courses and users in your LMS are configured with the appropriate data to support interdepartmental billing. Every relevant course must have a price and a sponsoring organization. This is the organization that licensed or developed the course and will receive payment whenever someone in another organization takes the course. Every employee in the LMS must be associated with the organization in which they work. This is the organization that will pay for the employee to take the course. Decide whether you want to transfer payment from the user's organization to the sponsoring organization when the user enrolls in the course, or when the user completes the course.

The next step is to make sure that the LMS provides a method to extract the information about course enrollment or completion status, the course price, the user's organization, and the course's sponsoring organization. These data may be accessible through the API, a scheduled report in Excel format, or some other method.

Finally, your IT group, your LMS vendor, or a third party will need to develop a program to extract the LMS data and, in the financial system's general ledger, debit course price from the user's organization and credit the sponsoring organization.

Data Warehouse

If your organization needs to provide reports on data from multiple systems, such as an LMS or knowledge management, social networking and collaboration, enterprise resource planning, or financial systems, your IT organization may have deployed a data warehouse. In this case, data are extracted from multiple systems and stored in a common database where the data can be combined, reported, and analyzed.

Typically, data can be exported from an LMS in either of two ways: the API provided with the LMS or a data export, which may be a scheduled report generated in a CSV or XML format.

* * *

LMS integration offers many benefits to LMS users, administrators, and the organization. Integration enables data sharing between systems, which streamlines the user experience and enhances data integrity. It can also be used to automate complex transactions, which reduces the risk of data entry errors and omissions. Your integration efforts will require programming support from your IT department or LMS vendor.

A close cousin to integration is data migration. While integration projects enable two or more systems to share and synchronize data on an ongoing basis, migration involves a one-time transfer of data from one system to another, in this case from your old LMS to your new one.

Step 4: Course and Data Migration

If you are changing LMS products or moving from a custom LMS to an off-the-shelf product, you will probably need to move the training data and courses from your legacy system to the new LMS. This is what course and data migration is all about, and it is one of the more technical tasks in an LMS implementation.

First, you will need to decide how much data to migrate and how to map the data from your old system to your new one. Then, you will need to work with your IT department, who will develop a migration software program. There is some "choreography" involved. The data must be migrated in three stages, in a specific sequence at each stage.

If your IT department is not equipped to support you, you will need to get support from your vendors. Your legacy LMS vendor may be best positioned to pull the data out of your old LMS. Your new LMS vendor can help with importing the data into the new LMS.

Ask This

Ask your new LMS vendor to help with importing data into the new LMS.

Deciding How Much Data to Migrate

The first step is to decide how much data to migrate. A good practice is to move as little data as possible. The more data you migrate, the greater potential for errors and problems that may delay your implementation project. Check with your IT and legal departments; they may already have an information retention policy for your organization, which you can use to guide your decision.

Suppose your organization has been using its former LMS for the last 10 years. All the employee training records for those 10 years are stored in the old system. After checking with IT and legal, you find out that your organization's policy is to retain employment records for three years. So rather than migrating all the data from your old LMS, you decide to migrate just the data from the last three years. You ask IT or your LMS vendor to create a database archive of all older data so that if the need arises, you can ask them to restore the backup long enough for you to run a report. Archiving the data is not difficult; IT probably archives databases and puts them into "deep storage" all the time. Because the older data are not immediately accessible in your LMS, archived data may take several days to retrieve from deep storage, but the removal of older data keeps your LMS clean and simplifies your implementation project.

Ask This

Ask your IT and legal departments if they have already established an information retention policy for your organization.

There may be some exceptions to the policy. Let's say you have a course, Advanced Inventory Management, that has a prerequisite course, Basic Inventory Management. Before people are allowed to take the advanced course, they must complete the basic one. In this case, you may want to migrate the last five years of course completion data for the prerequisite basic course. This will allow anyone who has completed the basic course in the last five years to take the advanced course.

Another exception to the policy may be compliance and certification courses. Suppose you offer a certification course. Upon completing the course, a person becomes certified. The certification expires after four years, at which time they must take another course to be recertified. In this case, you should migrate the last four years of course completion data for the certification course so that you can maintain proof of certification for anyone who earned their certification three or four years ago.

The amount of data you migrate affects how long the data migration process takes, from programming to execution, testing, and validation. To streamline your LMS implementation process and lower the risk of errors, migrate only the data that are absolutely needed. Use this rationale, along with your organization's broader data retention policies, to counter objections from team members who think all legacy data should be migrated to the new LMS.

Mapping the Data

As you begin to plan the migration of your legacy data to the new LMS, you will need to do some data mapping. Create a spreadsheet or table listing the data fields in the old LMS and how they correspond, or map, to fields in the new LMS. Do this for user data, course data, and user-course status data.

Your data map will ensure that the data extracted from your old system are placed in the appropriate location in the new LMS. As you develop your data map, you will need to address any incompatibilities between the way the data and courses were stored in the legacy system versus the new LMS.

Your data map should include the field type, such as text, number, or date, and the field length for each data field in the old LMS so that you can map it to an appropriate data field of the same type in your new system. Table 8-1 shows an example of a data map for migrating data from an old LMS to a new one.

Table 8-1. Data Map Example

Category	Old LMS			New LMS			Migration Rules
	Field Name	Required	Type	Field Name	Required	Type	
User Data	UserID	Yes	Char(20)	UserUniqueID	Yes	Char(50)	
	Login	Yes	Char(30)	Username	Yes	Char(50)	
	Password	Yes	Char(30)	Password	Yes	Char(50)	
				Prefix	No	Char(6)	
	FirstName	Yes	Char(20)	FirstName	Yes	Char(20)	
	MiddleInit	No	Char(1)	MiddleName	No	Char(20)	
	LastName	Yes	Char(20)	LastName	Yes	Char(30)	
				Suffix	No	Char(6)	

Category	Old LMS			New LMS			Migration Rules
	Field Name	Required	Type	Field Name	Required	Type	
	Email	Yes	Char(50)	EmailAddress	Yes	Valid Email Address	Data from old LMS email field will be lost if not fully qualified email address. Required field cannot be left blank, so populate with EnterYour EmailAddress Here@ company.com.
	Phone	No	Char(12)	OfficePhone	No	Valid Phone Number	Data from old LMS phone field will be lost if not fully qualified phone number. Some users may have entered their cell numbers here.
				CellPhone	No	Valid Phone Number	

Pay attention to the length of text fields, like the course description, to ensure that the text coming from the old system is not truncated when entered into the new LMS. If the text is too long for the new LMS, decide whether to edit the text down to the appropriate length before or after you move it. Table 8-2 shows an example of old LMS data that are too long for the new LMS.

Table 8-2. Example of Old LMS Data Too Long for the New LMS

Course Description in Old LMS (Too Long for New LMS)	This course is designed to be taken by new and experienced managers who have difficulty delegating tasks that could be performed by members of their staff. If you find yourself working before or after hours quite often and you notice that your direct reports have all gone home already, you may be having problems delegating. When you spend time doing things that others could be doing, you may not have time for the things that only you can do. If this situation sounds familiar, you should consider taking this course, where you will learn and practice using effective techniques to identify tasks that could be delegated, decide who on your team is best suited to the tasks, determine how much supervision you need to provide, define checkpoints to monitor progress, and give feedback to those people to whom you have delegated work.
Course Description Truncated Due to Smaller Field Size in New LMS	This course is designed to be taken by new and experienced managers who have difficulty delegating tasks that could be performed by members of their staff. If you find yourself working before or after hours quite often and you notice that your direct reports have all gone home already, you may be having problems delegating. When you spend time doing things that others could be doing, you may not have time for the things that only you can do. If this situation sounds familiar, you
Course Description Rewritten to Conform to Field Size in New LMS	This course is for managers who need to develop their delegating skills. Spending time doing things others could be doing leaves less time for the things that only you can do. In this course, you will learn effective techniques to identify tasks that could be delegated, decide who on your team is best suited to the tasks, determine how much supervision you need to provide, define checkpoints to monitor progress, and give feedback to those people to whom you have delegated work.

Sometimes, data mapping requires some creative problem solving. For example, your old LMS may have stored each user's manager as an email address, while the new LMS may store the manager's user ID. In this case, you will need to find a way to identify manager user IDs from their email addresses in the legacy data to populate that field in the new system.

Your new LMS may enforce stricter data integrity rules than your legacy system. For example, let's say that some of the courses in your legacy system were entered in such a way that their end date was earlier than their start date. The old LMS did not have a problem with this anomaly, but the new LMS has built-in rules to ensure the integrity of the data and will not accept these courses. In a situation like this, you would need to adjust the dates in the old system before moving them to the new LMS.

You may find opportunities to normalize the data from your old LMS. Normalization is a best practice for good data design, because it reduces data redundancy and improves data integrity. For example, some fields may have been entered as text in the old system, but they can be implemented as a drop-down list of predefined values in the new LMS. Using predefined values, wherever appropriate, improves data consistency, making it easier to use data in reports. In this case, you will need to clean up the old data so that each text value can be mapped to the appropriate predefined drop-down list value in the new system. You may also find that you were keeping track of the same information in multiple fields in the old system, which can lead to errors and inconsistencies.

Your IT organization will likely have the skills to help you find opportunities to normalize and improve your data as you map the data from your old LMS to the new one. Use the IT architect on your implementation team, or someone from IT, as a resource.

Migrating User Data

Once you have decided how much data to move and mapped your data to the new LMS, you are ready to get started with your data migration.

LMS data must be migrated in a specific sequence. First, the user accounts and profile data must be loaded into the system. Next, the course content and descriptive data are loaded. The last step is migrating the transcript data. Transcript data describe the relationship between users and courses, so the users and courses must already be in place before the transcript data are loaded.

If you have decided to integrate the LMS with a system that manages user accounts, as described earlier in this chapter under step 3, the feed must be developed, implemented, and tested before you migrate anything else.

To develop your user data feed, you must:

1. Decide what user profile data fields you want in the new LMS.
2. Identify the source system where these data originate, such as a human resource management system.
3. Create a data map that contains the names of all these fields in the originating system and the corresponding field names in the LMS. Your IT department will refer to this data map when they write a program to extract the data from the originating system.
4. Ask your LMS vendor to provide documentation on the user data import file format that your IT department will need to follow. Your IT department will refer to the LMS file format documentation as they continue to write the program that transforms the extracted data into the appropriate format and loads them into the LMS.
5. Your IT department will create a program, called a feed or an ETL process.
6. Your IT department will work with your LMS vendor to test the feed and ensure that it is working properly. You will need to compare the user profiles for several users in the new LMS with those in the old LMS to make sure the data are valid.
7. Because the data in your HR system are constantly changing, your IT department will work with your LMS vendor to schedule the feed to run automatically on a recurring basis.

In the event that you have no other system to supply your user data, then instead of a feed, you will need to migrate the user data from your old LMS.

To migrate user data from an old LMS, you must:

1. Decide what user profile data fields you want in the new LMS.
2. Create a data map that contains the names of all these fields in the old LMS and the corresponding field names in the new LMS. Your IT department will refer to this data map when they write a program to extract the data from the old LMS.
3. Ask your LMS vendor to provide documentation on the user data import file format that your IT department will need to follow. Your IT department will refer to the LMS file format documentation as they continue to write the program that transforms the extracted data into the appropriate format and loads them into the LMS.
4. Your IT department will create a program, called a feed or an ETL process.

5. Your IT department will work with your LMS vendor to test the feed and ensure that it is working properly. You will need to spot-check the user profiles of several users in the system to make sure the data are valid.
6. Because the old LMS will be retired, this is a one-time process. Going forward, you will need to enable new users to create accounts directly in the new LMS.

Migrating Standards-Based Courseware

The courseware migration process depends on the type of LMS and the courseware standards.

If you are moving from one academic LMS to another, you will need to export your course to the appropriate format for your new LMS and then import it. The IMS Global Learning Consortium® has developed a number of standards for doing this, including the Common Cartridge®, LTI®, and QTI® standards, all covered in chapter 5. Check to see whether your legacy and new LMS support these standards. It will make course migration between academic LMS products a lot easier.

If you are moving from one corporate LMS to another, the process can be a bit more complex.

If you have implemented SCORM-based courses, you will need to reinstall the SCORM package for each of the courses on your new LMS. When courses are developed and exported to SCORM, a zipped file (.zip) is generated containing all the course files. This zipped file is called a SCORM package. Some LMS products provide a batch method that enables you to queue up the installation of multiple SCORM course packages. Other LMS products will require you install one SCORM course package at a time.

Even though the SCORM courses may have worked well on your legacy system, they may need some adjustment to work optimally on the new LMS.

For SCORM courses, you will need to:

1. Inventory your existing courses, as well as those in your development pipeline.
2. Categorize the courses by the authoring tool or vendor that produced them.
3. Install and thoroughly test one course from each category. Test course launch, player compatibility, bookmarking, navigation, audio, video, animations, graphics, and embedded links, as well as test scoring and module and page tracking. Make sure the course shows up properly in the transcript of the new LMS.
4. If you run into problems, make any needed adjustments to the course or SCORM manifest, reinstall, and retest.

5. Replicate your adjustments to all other courses in the category; install and test them all.
6. Manage an exception list of any courses that don't work properly. If you no longer have the source code for the course, you may need to redevelop the course using a more compatible authoring tool.

> Whenever you hire a vendor to create an e-learning course, always require them to deliver the source files at the end of the project. Keep the source files for all your custom courses, including those developed by vendors and those developed in-house. Create a "readme" file that documents the authoring tools and version numbers with which the course was created. In the event you need to make changes, this approach will allow you to author the course in the associated authoring tool, revise the images in the associated photo and graphics editing tool, and edit any videos and audio tracks in the associated media editing tools.

For courseware developed around a specification other than SCORM, the process is likely to be easier; however, there are still some risks.

For AICC courses, you will need to:

1. Move any courses hosted on your old LMS to the new LMS or a separate file server. Engage your IT department for help with this.
2. Change the course launch URLs in your new LMS to the address of the new file server. Hopefully, any URLs that are embedded in your courses are relative rather than fully qualified. Relative URLs are without the domain name for your LMS—for example, /images/logo.jpg—while fully qualified URLs include the domain name—for example, http://myoldlms.com/images/logo.jpg. Relative URLs will not need to be changed.
3. If after moving your AICC courses and testing them you see a lot of "page not found" or "page cannot be displayed" errors, then you may have fully qualified URLs in your course that need to be changed.

Experience API and cmi5 are newer specifications. Increasingly, organizations are deploying courses using these standards instead of SCORM. A best practice is to host your content on a file server that is separate from the LMS. Doing so will require fewer URL adjustments and make migrating to a new LMS much easier. However, the reality is that many organizations upload their cmi5 courses to the LMS in a way similar to SCORM content. In this case, migrating cmi5 courses to a new LMS will require a process similar to migrating SCORM.

For cmi5 courses, you will need to:

1. Upload each cmi5 course to the new LMS, which will generate a unique ID for the course.
2. Extract the LMS course information, such as course title, description, and transactional data, from your old system, replace the legacy unique identifier with the new one, and import your data into the new LMS.
3. The cmi5 specification is based on xAPI, so in addition to the LMS-generated data, there are course-generated tracking data stored in a learning record store. If you are using a third-party LRS and plan to continue using it in conjunction with your new LMS, you don't need to change anything. However, if your new LMS has its own embedded LRS, you may want to change the cmi5 course configuration to point to the new LRS. This is done by changing the "Publisher Unique Identifier" in the cmi5 .xml file. Ask your IT partners for help with this if needed.
4. Check with your own xAPI and cmi5 course developers and your LMS and LRS vendors to determine what must be done. Then test it with a few courses first to make sure your process is working effectively, before moving the remaining courses.

> Testing your e-learning courses can take time, especially if you have a lot of them. But it is better for you to find the bugs and fix them in advance of going live, rather than getting calls from people who are trying to complete the courses after the new system has been implemented. This will be covered in more depth in chapter 9.

Migrating Course Data

There are course-related data in the LMS for all courses, regardless of whether they are webinars, classroom, or self-paced. These course-related data include a unique course ID, course title, description, schedule, locations, instructors, metadata, credits, and more.

If you're implementing an academic LMS that supports the IMS Global Learning Consortium standards, your course data can be transferred using the Common Cartridge, LTI, and QTI specifications. Work with your old LMS vendor to extract the data and your new vendor to import them.

For a corporate LMS, you must:

1. Decide what course data fields you want in the new LMS.
2. Create a data map that contains the names of all these fields in the old LMS and the corresponding field names in the new LMS. Your IT department will refer to this data map when they write a program to extract the data from the old LMS.
3. Ask your LMS vendor to provide documentation on the course data import file format that your IT department will need to follow. Your IT department will refer to the LMS file format documentation as they continue to write the program that transforms the extracted data into the appropriate format and loads them into the LMS.
4. Your IT department will create a program, called a feed or an ETL process.
5. Edit the data file extracted from your old LMS and replace the legacy course unique IDs for all SCORM and cmi5 courses with the new unique IDs that were established when you installed the SCORM course in the new LMS. This can be done manually or programmatically as part of the data transformation process.
6. Your IT department will work with your LMS vendor to test the feed and ensure that it is working properly. You will need to compare the course details pages of several courses in the new LMS with those in the old LMS to make sure the data are valid.
7. Because the old LMS will be retired, this is a one-time process. Going forward, you will need to enable administrators to create new courses directly in the new LMS.

In case you are wondering why you must edit the data file, here is the reason: You cannot simply move SCORM or cmi5 course packages from an old LMS to a new LMS. The course packages must be installed in the new LMS. The installation process provides the LMS with information about the course contents that is required for effective SCORM or cmi5 interoperability with the LMS. When you install a SCORM or cmi5 course on your new LMS, a new unique identifier is generated. At this point, the SCORM course is present in the new LMS, but some of the course-related LMS data are still missing. If you skip step 5, a duplicate course will be created in your new LMS using the old LMS's unique identifier. This duplicate course will contain the course description and other course-related data, but it will be disconnected from the actual SCORM course.

Migrating Transcript Data

Once you have added users and courses to your new LMS, the last step is to move your legacy transcript data to the new system. Transcripts represent the relationship between users and courses, which is why the users and courses must be present in the system before you move the transcript data. Remember to migrate the least amount of historical data necessary based on your organization's data retention policy.

To migrate transcript data, you must:

1. Decide what transcript data fields you want in the new LMS.
2. Create a data map that contains the names of all these fields in the old LMS and the corresponding field names in the new LMS. Your IT department will refer to this data map when they write a program to extract the data from the old LMS.
3. Ask your LMS vendor to provide documentation on the transcript data import file format that your IT department will need to follow. Your IT department will refer to the LMS file format documentation as they continue to write the program that transforms the extracted data into the appropriate format and loads them into the LMS.
4. Your IT department will create a program, called a feed or an ETL process.
5. Your IT department will work with your LMS vendor to test the feed and ensure that it is working properly. You will need to compare the transcripts for several users in the new LMS with those in the old LMS to make sure the data are valid.
6. Because the old LMS will be retired, this is a one-time process. Going forward, you will need to enable administrators to create new courses directly in the new LMS.

Migration Stages

The user, course, and transcript migrations should be performed in three stages:

1. Migrate a relatively small sample of data and test the process.
2. Migrate all data to date prior to user acceptance testing.
3. After user acceptance testing is complete, migrate the data that have been added or changed between stage 2 and going live.

Clearly, you'll want to avoid any data loss, so the first stage is to migrate a relatively small sample of the data and test it to verify that the migration programming is working properly.

The second stage is to migrate all the current data. Once this is done, you will be able to enhance the course setups by configuring any features and functionality that you may not have had in your old LMS and perform user acceptance testing.

The third stage happens just prior to going live, when you will transfer the data that have been added or changed since the full migration you performed in the second stage. You may want to manage separate "blackout" periods, one where LMS administrators do not add new courses or classes, and another when end users do not register. These blackouts will help ensure that your data migration is thorough and will avoid administrator rework, but you will want to minimize the length of each blackout period to avoid disrupting your training operations too much. More information about how to manage these and other steps related to going live are described in chapter 9.

Key Takeaways

This chapter focused on steps 3 and 4 of the implementation process: systems integration and data migration. The key takeaways are:

- LMS products are often integrated with systems that manage user accounts and profiles such as the human resource management system used by a business, the member management system used by a professional association, or the student information system used by an academic institution.
- Implementing a single sign-on solution streamlines the user experience for people who have already logged in to the organization's network, allowing their login credentials to be passed to the LMS automatically so that they do not need to log in again.
- LMS products may also be integrated with portals, enterprise search tools, a company's general ledger, or a data warehouse.
- There are many ways to integrate LMS systems, including data feeds, application programming interfaces, and deep links to specific LMS webpages.
- When replacing an old LMS with a new one, the training data from the old system must be migrated to the new LMS. This process must be done sequentially and repeated in three different stages.
- A guiding principle is to move as little data as possible to reduce risk and speed the implementation process.

- To migrate data from your old LMS to your new one, you will need to create a map of the data fields across the two systems and compensate for differences in field types, character lengths, and data integrity rules.
- Moving standards-based e-learning courseware can be tricky and must be coordinated with the training data migration process. Different procedures are required to move SCORM, AICC, and cmi5 courseware.

This chapter introduced the types of systems integrations you may need to position your LMS in the broader IT technology infrastructure. We have also covered all the processes involved in moving your data and content from a legacy system to your new LMS.

The next chapter covers the final steps of the implementation process: testing and going live.

CHAPTER 9

Testing Your LMS and Going Live

This chapter applies to all three types of LMS products. It covers the final steps of the LMS implementation process. It explains how to test the system to make sure it is working properly so that you can fix any problems before they affect your users. It also lists steps you can follow as you plan to go live with your new LMS.

As discussed in the previous two chapters, LMS implementation typically involves six major steps. This chapter covers the final two steps, testing and going live.

Figure 9-1. The 6 Steps of LMS Implementation: Testing and Going Live

After all the work you've done planning, configuring, integrating, and migrating your content to your new LMS, you are probably very eager to get the new system up and running for your users. Don't rush; you're at a critical point. Many organizations do not provide adequate time in the project schedule for testing and debugging the system. If there are bugs in the system configuration, data, content, or integrations and you do not catch them before going live, your help desk may be overwhelmed with calls. Your users and sponsors may have a negative reaction to the system.

There are many administrator and user features to be tested, so you'll need to be methodical and thorough. You can start planning your testing effort early in the implementation project in parallel with other tasks, but the testing itself happens at the end of the project, just before going live.

Planning your go live process is also critically important. Going live involves a sequence of steps that must be carefully mapped out and followed. To ensure success and a smooth transition to your new LMS, you will need to anticipate potential problems and determine how to mitigate them in advance so that you can respond quickly to any problems that emerge.

Step 5: User Acceptance Testing

The last major step before going live with your LMS is to conduct user acceptance testing, or UAT, as shortened in the product development world. In this case, your organization is the "user," and you are testing the LMS to make sure the vendor has delivered a fully working, bug-free system. You are also testing to make sure your configuration, courses, and data are available and working properly in the system. Your testing continues until you are satisfied, at which point you are essentially "accepting" the system from the vendor.

The key to user acceptance testing is to be thorough in testing every part of the system. Your goal is to find and correct bugs before you go live. Keep in mind that your users will be affected by any bugs that you miss during this phase. When people have a bad experience in the first few weeks or months after the LMS is introduced, their trust in the system and in your organization can be damaged. It can be very difficult to recover from that. All the time and effort you put into discovering and correcting bugs in the system before you go live will be well worth it.

Start by convening the core team to brainstorm a list of procedures to test. Include all the procedures your team can think of: those performed by administrators, learners, report users, instructors, and any other security roles you have defined. Table 9-1 provides some examples of learner, instructor, and administrator procedures to be tested.

Table 9-1. Example List of LMS Procedures to Test

Learner Test Script Examples	Instructor Test Script Examples	Administrator Test Script Examples
• Find a course by browsing the catalog. • Find a course by searching. • Register for a classroom course. • Register for a webinar. • Complete a SCORM course. • Complete an assessment. • Complete a survey. • Complete assigned training. • Complete certification training. • View the transcript. • Print a course completion certificate.	• Schedule a class. • View a roster. • Print a sign-in sheet. • View a gradebook. • Take attendance. • Reschedule a class and notify registrants. • Cancel a class and notify registrants.	• Create a classroom course with a wait list. • Create a webinar course. • Install a SCORM course. • Create an assessment. • Create a survey. • Update a course. • Install a new version of a SCORM course. • Deactivate a course. • Run a report. • Create an audience. • Assign a course to an audience.

Once you have your list of procedures to test, you will need to develop a test script for each procedure. Divide the list among team members. There is likely to be a large amount of work to be done here, so you may want to engage some of the extended team. Ask each team member to run through the procedure and make a note of every action performed: menu items selected, fields entered, checkboxes checked, buttons pushed, and so on.

You can provide a spreadsheet format for the test planners to use and create a worksheet for each test. Each worksheet may include a header with the test name, the role of the person executing the test (administrator, instructor, student, and so on), and any requisite data required to be configured in the system to run the test. For example, if your test specifies that a student find a course and register for it, the student's account and the course must both be present in the system. The rows in the worksheet may represent the steps in the procedure. You may want to include three columns to represent a description of the action to be taken, a description of the expected result, and a place for the tester to enter the actual result. Table 9-2 illustrates an example of a test script format, where the tester would fill in the column labeled *Actual Result*.

Table 9-2. Example Test Script

Test Name: Register for a Classroom Course
Tester Role: Learner

	Action	**Expected Result**	**Actual Result**
1	Enter the search string "Leadership" and click the search button.	A list of courses about leadership appears in the search results.	
2	Select "Leadership 101."	The course details page is displayed.	
3	Click the register button.	A list of class offerings is displayed.	
4	Select the class offering for January 3.	The registration "are you sure" page is displayed.	
5	Click the yes button.	The registration confirmation page is displayed.	
6	Check your email inbox.	A registration confirmation email notification is received within a few minutes.	
7	Open the registration confirmation email message.	Your name, the course name, the class date, and the location are listed. A calendar invitation is attached.	
8	Open the attached calendar invitation.	The calendar invitation opens in Outlook.	
9	Accept the calendar invitation.	The class is added to your Outlook calendar.	

After all test procedure scripts have been defined and documented, identify resources to perform the testing and create a test schedule. Here, you will want to involve extended team members. Assign relevant test procedures to team members based on their role in relation to the LMS. The tests they perform will begin to acclimate them to the new system, increasing their proficiency and confidence in using the system before you go live. You may want to schedule no more than one or two hours of testing per day for each tester so that they can continue to perform other work duties.

Your test cases will require specific data to be set up in the system. Do your best to execute the tests in a logical order to make test setup easier:

- Test 1: Administrator creates a course.
- Test 2: Student registers for the course.
- Test 3: Instructor marks student complete.
- Test 4: Student views transcript.
- Test 5: Administrator runs a completion report for the course.Establish a spreadsheet or database for compiling and tracking all the bugs your testers find. Alternatively, consider using a commercial bug-tracking system. There are several good ones available in the cloud, which you can license for use during your user acceptance testing phase. Ask your IT department whether they already have one in place that you can use. These systems allow multiple users to check and update the status of bugs, run reports, receive notifications, and so on. Depending on the number of people involved, a single person tracking the bugs in a spreadsheet can work equally well.

Ask This

Ask your IT department whether they have a bug-tracking system in place that you can use.

To manage the bugs uncovered in your testing:

1. Assign a test lead to debrief testers and record bugs in the tracking system.
2. Convene the core team at the end of each testing day to discuss the status of all newly found and open bugs. It's important to meet this often to process bugs expeditiously.

3. Prioritize each bug as critical (must be fixed immediately; prevents further testing); moderate (must be fixed prior to going live); or low (should be fixed in a future release).
4. Route bugs appropriately:
   » Route bugs related to the content and course data to the appropriate course developers in your organization.
   » Route bugs related to scheduling, location, instructor, and configuration data to your LMS administrators.
   » Route bugs related to the system to your IT organization or the vendor.
5. Keep track of who owns each bug at any given point until it is corrected.

> Be sure that you always retest corrected bugs to verify that they have been fixed. A common problem occurs when a bug is reported as fixed and you find out later that the bug description had been misunderstood and the bug was actually not fixed, or the way in which the bug was fixed had introduced new bugs.

Once all tests have been completed and all critical and moderate bugs have been fixed, you are ready to go live with your new LMS. I have seen many situations where organizations had to postpone the target go live date until user acceptance testing was satisfactorily completed. While not ideal, this delay ultimately benefits the organization by going live with a fully tested and stable LMS that users can rely on.

Step 6: Go Live

The final step is to go live with your new LMS. Many organizations use IT jargon by referring to the date they go live as *GoLive* or *Day One.* To prepare for going live, it is a good idea to meet with the core team to brainstorm a list of risks and a contingency plan to mitigate each risk. Notify your course owners and administrators well in advance of the go live date. Advise them to avoid scheduling critical training during the week before and the week after the go live date, if possible. Release the appropriate communications to your sponsors, extended team members, and end users to ensure that everyone is aware and expectations are set.

Preparing the Users and Administrators

LMS products must strike a balance between offering robust functionality and being easy to use. Due to the many ways they are used by various organizations, most systems are complex enough that they require some training, particularly for administrators. During your user acceptance testing effort, you may have identified some administrative procedures that could benefit from a job aid, an administrator guide, or hands-on training. You should prepare and distribute training materials and schedule training activities prior to going live. Some of the organizations I worked with have scheduled weekly or biweekly LMS administrator web conferences, where the LMS screen is shared and advanced features are demonstrated, time-saving shortcuts are introduced, and emerging questions and concerns are discussed.

You may also consider creating short videos or systems simulations to orient first-time users to the basic system features, capabilities, and navigation. You can make these self-paced tutorials available on the LMS homepage.

While many LMS users may prefer to explore and learn to use the system on their own, others may prefer to learn through a tutorial or hands-on training. While this type of training is not always necessary for a new LMS implementation, it can be very helpful in getting the organization up to speed quickly, minimizing disruption, and helping to increase user satisfaction.

Preparing the Help Desk

When planning how to resolve any issues end users of your LMS may encounter, it may be helpful for you to think in terms of a tiered support structure. Tier one is your help desk. This is the front line; your help desk responds directly to user inquiries. The help desk may operate during business hours, extended hours, or around the clock. It may be accessible through the phone, email, or online chat. Check with your IT organization on how they provide help desk support for other enterprise systems. They may have staff, procedures, and help desk software that can be used to support your LMS.

Tier two typically consists of LMS administrators who troubleshoot problems that cannot be resolved by tier one. If tier two cannot resolve the problem, they will probably know how to direct it to someone who can.

Ask This

Check with your IT organization on how they provide help desk support for other enterprise systems.

Tier three may consist of several different groups, each responsible for its own set of issues. For example, the LMS vendor is responsible for system errors and other malfunctions; your IT organization may be responsible for problems with the network, single sign-on, or data feeds; and your e-learning course developers may be responsible for bugs in a specific online course. The idea behind a tiered structure is that most of the user issues get resolved at tier one, while more complex problems are escalated to the appropriate tier.

Many LMS vendors provide support to your administrators, but not to end users. You may need to provide your own help desk or contract with a third party to respond to questions and problems reported by people who take courses in your LMS. If so, you will need to prepare the help desk to resolve as many issues as possible, so that fewer problems are passed up the chain to your administrators. In the IT world, the service expected from your help desk beginning on the go live date is called day one support.

Consider providing a help desk script to your support staff. Create a list of anticipated call topics and describe how to respond to each one, including questions to ask, information to record, and solutions to suggest. Some examples include how to get to the LMS, how to recover a lost password, what to do if something does not appear in your transcript, how to register for a course, and so on. Provide an escalation process for issues your help desk staff cannot resolve, including whom to contact for any given issue and what information to collect from the user (such as username, email address, phone number, date and time the problem occurred, steps to reproduce the problem, screenshot, and the error message) before escalating a problem.

Before you go live, meet with your help desk staff to walk through the help desk script and answer any questions they may have. Provide them with access to the LMS and demonstrate the resolution procedures for any issues that may require them to use the system. Some LMS products provide a way for help desk staff to "impersonate" a user in the system to see exactly what the user sees. Introduce this and other relevant features to the help desk staff. The more familiar they are with the LMS prior to the go live date, the more helpful they can be to your end users.

The Blackout Period

As mentioned in the "Migration Stages" section of chapter 8, you will need to migrate data from your old LMS to your new LMS in three stages. The first stage is a test of the data migration process with just a sample of data. The second stage is a full data migration, after which user acceptance testing is performed. This testing can take several weeks, and during that time, people will continue taking courses and generating new data on your old LMS. So the final data migration stage occurs during the end user blackout period, when the old LMS is deactivated so that no one can use it and any new or changed data are migrated one last time. This is called a delta data migration because it only involves the difference between the state of data in your old LMS between the second and third data migrations.

While you're performing the final, delta data migration, make sure that neither your old system nor the new LMS is available to end users so that no more data are generated or changed. During this "blackout" period, you will want to shut down your old LMS, perform the delta data migration, spot-check the data and functionality in the new LMS, and redirect the legacy system's web address to the new LMS. If anything goes wrong, you should be prepared to reactivate the old system and postpone your go live date until the problem is diagnosed and resolved.

Some organizations plan for two blackout periods: the one described previously for end users, and another for administrators. The administrator blackout occurs after the second data migration and lasts until going live. Its purpose is to limit the delta data migration to transactional data, which speeds the go live process and reduces risk of errors and data loss by eliminating the need for course data migration and simplifying go live testing. During an administrator blackout, LMS administrators are instructed not to add new courses, change or deactivate existing courses, or schedule new classes in the old LMS. This can be accomplished in some organizations with adequate up-front planning and expectation setting. For other organizations where the pace of training is rapid, an administrator blackout is not practical.

To minimize disruption to your end users, you may want to schedule the end user blackout and final go live tasks to occur over a weekend, assuming that the resources involved in your go live process are available.

Key Takeaways

This chapter focused on the final two steps of the implementation process: user acceptance testing and going live. The key takeaways are:

- User acceptance testing involves thorough, methodical end-to-end testing of all learner and administrator features of the LMS. This is where you, the customer, make sure the LMS is configured, loaded, and operating exactly the way you expect—before you go live!
- There are a number of things you must do to plan your user acceptance testing efforts, including identifying and documenting test cases, preparing testing worksheets, scheduling the tests, and assigning people to perform them.
- As your organization executes the user acceptance testing process, you will need to meet at the end of each day to inventory, document, prioritize, and route bugs that are found. You can create your own bug-tracking spreadsheets or use a commercial bug-management system.
- You must update the status of bugs as they are reported and fixed. Even after a bug is declared "fixed," you must be sure it is retested and the fix is confirmed. You may also need to rerun some of your test cases to make sure that fixing one bug didn't introduce other bugs.
- Going live involves some critical steps that must happen in a prescribed sequence. You will need to work with your team to anticipate things that might go wrong and how to mitigate them.
- You must prepare your users, administrators, and help desk in advance of going live.

Once your LMS has gone live, you need to properly organize your LMS operations. The next chapter will focus on getting the most from your LMS with standards, policies, processes, and governance.

CHAPTER 10

Operating Your LMS With Standards and Governance

This chapter applies mostly to corporate LMS and LCMS-LMS products. It describes the policies, procedures, conventions, and other standards that you need to establish to get the most out of your LMS. It covers taxonomy design for your catalog and metadata and how to document and manage changes to your LMS configuration. Even if you've been using your LMS for months or years, this chapter explains how to manage content cleanup and system housekeeping. It also covers something that many organizations lack, a governance structure for managing LMS decision making and operations.

Your organization may be about to spend, or may have already spent, a lot of time, effort, resources, and money on acquiring and implementing (or updating) an LMS. It is important to protect this investment by establishing the necessary operations and governance measures to ensure that your system continues to be easy to use and provides highly relevant content to your end users. By putting these critical pieces into place, you are much more likely to get optimum value from your LMS.

Too often, organizations operate their LMS for several years without adequate standards, policies, processes, and governance. The result is a giant L-M-*Mess*. Just recently, I worked with an organization whose LMS contained hundreds of unused courses, including one on how to use Windows 98. Don't let this happen to you! Make sure you have established standards, in this case a content life-cycle policy and review process.

After you first install your LMS, you can expect it to grow and change. Your organization's needs will evolve, more content will be added, users and administrators will come and go, new groups of users may become engaged, new features will be enabled, and some features you think will be useful now may never be used.

I have worked with too many organizations whose legacy LMS contains outdated courses, a haphazard organizing structure, duplicate user accounts, catalog dead ends, a lack of accountability or course ownership, inconsistent naming and numbering conventions, reporting anomalies, a lack of distinction in course titles and descriptions, unused features, and spam-like email notifications. Does any of this sound familiar? If you think you may be heading this way or you're already there, this chapter is for you.

If your organization is implementing a brand-new LMS for the first time, then now is a good idea to take steps to avoid these problems.

If your organization is planning to migrate to a new LMS or undertake a major upgrade of your current product, you can take advantage of this opportunity to clean up and optimize your content and then, while the organization is still mobilized around the LMS project, take steps to ensure your new system doesn't end up in the same state as your old one.

Even if you are planning to stick with your existing product for the next few years, there are steps you can take to clean things up and manage LMS operations better going forward.

How to Optimize the Operation and Governance of Your LMS

As shown in Figure 10-1, there five major areas you must address. Don't think of these areas as sequential steps. You can start anywhere, as long as you attend to all five, which are equally important. If you do this, your organization will gain the most benefit from its LMS.

Figure 10-1. 5 Areas to Optimize Your LMS Operations

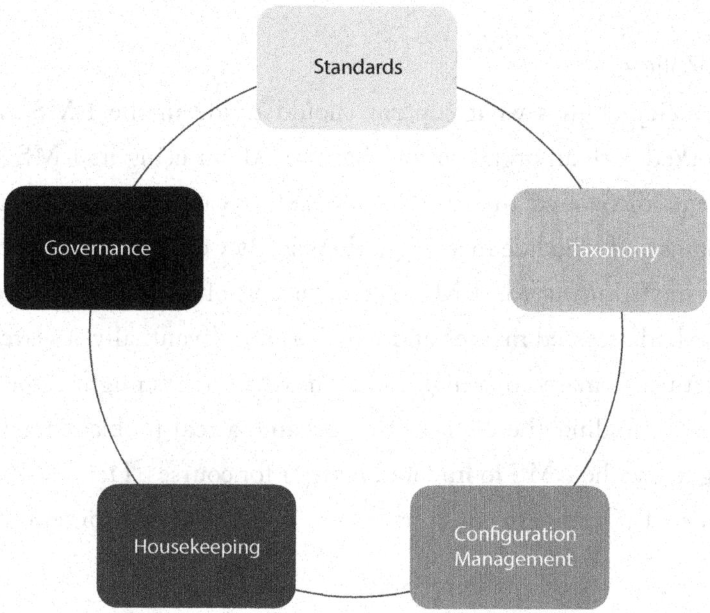

Standards

If your company website had no standards, its logos and layouts might vary from page to page, its many fonts and colors might resemble a ransom note, and its indecipherable mix of current and outdated information might cause considerable confusion. Customers would quickly decide not to do business with this disorganized company. The same is true of your LMS.

LMS standards include policies, procedures, guidelines, conventions, and consistent use of course properties and structures. These standards ensure that all administrators and stakeholders are using the LMS in the same fundamental way, which in turn makes it easier to use and manage.

Following are several standards to consider. Some examples are included, but they are not intended for you to cut and paste into your organization's implementation documentation. You will need to define standards that are unique and appropriate to the way you manage learning.

Policies

Policies provide a set of rules that all LMS administrators and stakeholders must follow. Your organization may define any number of policies. As a starting point, you should consider four common LMS policies: content inclusion, content ownership, content life cycle, and training data retention.

Content Inclusion Policy

A content inclusion policy defines what content should reside in the LMS and what content should not. I once worked with an organization that started out using its LMS for training. But, when other departments discovered the system's scheduling capabilities, they started using it to reserve conference rooms and schedule meetings. Then, as they discovered its tracking and reporting capabilities, they started using the LMS to deliver corporate communications. They would run reports to see who had accessed memos and who had not. Eventually, a search for a course on a given topic would return so many meetings and memos that users might scroll or page through hundreds of items before finding the course. This became a real problem for the organization. People gave up trying to use the LMS to find and register for courses. Help desk calls went up and enrollments went down. This problem could have been avoided with a content inclusion policy.

Example of a Content Inclusion Policy

To be included in the LMS, the learning program must:

- Support the organization's goals and strategic objectives.
- Be sponsored and funded by a department, function, or project team.
- Be offered in the appropriate languages, based on the needs of the target population.
- Be available in the appropriate delivery methods, based on the needs of the target population.

Items to be excluded from the LMS include:

- messages, announcements, policy statements, and other communications that are not learning programs
- meetings and other events that are not learning programs.

Content Ownership Policy

One of the chief complaints from organizations with outdated content in their LMS is that, after the content is published, no one is responsible for it. These organizations lack a content ownership policy.

A content ownership policy defines the requirements for establishing and tracking ownership of each learning activity in the LMS. It ensures that every active learning program has an owner. It defines the responsibilities that content owners have, how ownership should be passed from person to person, and what will happen to learning activities that have no owner.

Surprisingly, most of the organizations with which I have worked started out with no idea who owned the content in their LMS. No one was making sure the content was still up-to-date, relevant, accurate, and useful to the organization. Can you see the problem? Courses live in the LMS indefinitely. People might spend valuable time choosing a classroom course that sounds interesting, trying to register, and finding that there have been no offerings of this course in years. Even worse, people might spend hours completing an outdated self-paced course and learn all about old procedures that are no longer in use, information on products that no longer exist, or systems that don't work that way anymore. Misled customers, errors and omissions in work outputs, incorrectly performed tasks that must be redone, and mistakes that may never be discovered, but have a negative effect on productivity, liability, or employee and customer relations—who knows what additional harm this causes?

Example of a Content Ownership Policy

Every learning program must be assigned to an individual within the organization, who serves as the content owner. The content owner is responsible for ensuring the course is relevant, up-to-date, and accurate, and responding to learner inquiries related to the course and its content.

All course owners of active learning programs in the LMS are required to participate in scheduled content reviews and shelf-life management inventories. Content owners who do not participate will be notified, and, if no response is received within 30 days, their course(s) will be deactivated.

Active LMS courses that have no owner will be deactivated.

Content Life-Cycle Policy

A content life-cycle policy defines how often content should be reviewed and what criteria should be used for removing content from circulation.

Without such a content life-cycle policy, it is unlikely that people in your organization will review, update, and archive content when appropriate. This can result in outdated content remaining active in the LMS, introducing a risk that people may take an older version of the course, learn inaccurate information, or miss out on important updates. The presence of outdated courses in the course catalog and search results also makes it more difficult for users to find the most up-to-date and relevant content.

Given that many organizations don't keep track of who owns LMS content, there is typically no one who is responsible for managing the shelf life of the content. I have seen LMS implementations that contained self-paced courses as much as 20 years old. Alarmingly, people were occasionally taking those courses. Deactivating outdated courses makes the remaining content easier to find, increases people's trust in the system and its content, and ensures that you aren't distributing "bad" information.

Example of a Content Life-Cycle Policy

The life cycle of learning programs will be managed by monitoring usage, working with content owners to keep the programs up-to-date, and retiring courses that are no longer relevant. Content life-cycle review shall occur annually, at which time course registration reports will be run. Online courses with no registrations in the previous 12 months will be retired. Instructor-led courses with no scheduled offerings in the previous 12 months will be retired.

Training Data Retention Policy

A training data retention policy defines how long you will retain learner transcript data. If the LMS contains transcript data that are older than other nontraining data in your enterprise, you may not have established, implemented, or acted on your policy.

Most organizations have a broad-based enterprise information retention policy, which can provide guidance on how long you should retain training data. It may be shorter than you think. To find out more about your organization's information retention policy, check with your legal and IT departments.

Keep in mind that storing more data than called for by your information retention policy is not necessarily a bad thing. It does not usually affect LMS performance on the network or vendor hosting costs. Periodically clearing out your old data that are no longer needed is simply a good practice and sometimes makes reports easier to run, like clearing old files out of your filing cabinet.

Example of a Training Data Retention Policy

Learner training histories will be maintained in the LMS for five years and are accessible online, on demand through LMS transcripts and reports. Older training histories will be archived and can be accessed by request within a turnaround time of 12 weeks.

In some cases, learner records for some courses may be maintained for a longer period because the course is still recognized as a prerequisite for active courses, or it is associated with regulatory compliance or professional certification records that must be maintained for a longer timeframe.

Procedures

Without a clearly defined and documented set of procedures, your users may not know how to initiate a request, and your LMS administrators will be responding to every request separately. This can lead to a good deal of confusion, inefficiency, and inconsistency in how things are accomplished in the system. Procedures provide a clear path for users and administrators to follow as they work together to get things done with the LMS.

Procedures outline the steps administrators and content owners should follow when interacting with the LMS. Procedures may be supported by online request forms, documented workflows, roles and responsibilities, step-by-step instructions, and information to set expectations such as turnaround times, confirmations, and other communications.

Your organization may define any number of procedures. Some common ones include requesting a new learning program, updating or deactivating an existing learning program, adding or removing a training location, requesting a custom report, and requesting administrator permissions.

Think about all the things people will need from the LMS. How would you like them to interact with the system?

Examples of Procedures

Procedure to Cancel a Class

- Notify the class instructor that the class is canceled.
- Notify the classroom site manager that the class is canceled.
- Disable the class' ability to accept new registrations.
- Identify people who are already registered for the class.
- Send an email to all registrants informing them that the class is canceled, and include links to register for another class or withdraw from the course.
- Delete all registrations for the class, but keep their registrations in the course so that they have the option to register for another class offering.
- Deactivate the class.

Procedure to Request Administrator Access

- Complete the administrator access request form. Your request will be reviewed within two business days, and you will be notified of the outcome through email.
- If your request is approved, you can access the LMS as an administrator immediately. If your request is denied, you can contest the decision by contacting the LMS team leader at [contact info].

Guidelines

Guidelines provide a benchmark for administrators to use when entering information into the LMS. For example, you may provide guidelines related to creating titles and descriptions for learning programs. Think of this as a style guide, similar to one your organization may have for internal and external communications related to marketing, websites, and publications. In fact, you might even adopt this style guide and apply it to your LMS guidelines.

A clearly defined and documented set of guidelines, when used appropriately by administrators, makes the system easier to use. Names, titles, labels, icons, and other fields entered by administrators become more consistent and uniform. This improves the LMS user experience for everyone: learners and administrators.

Example of Guidelines for Entering Course Titles in an LMS

Course Titles

- Use a short title of six words or less, just long enough to accurately describe the learning program and distinguish it from other programs with similar titles.
- Search the LMS for other courses with similar titles and make sure your title is distinct.
- Avoid abbreviations and acronyms unless they are commonly known.
- Spell out words like *at* and *and* instead of using symbols like @ and & unless the symbol is part of a product or brand name.
- When the course is part of a series, ensure that all courses in the series are titled consistently.
- Use initial caps for all major words, as you might see in the title of a book or article.
- Be sure to check your spelling.

Conventions

Conventions are used to ensure the consistent application of data entered by administrators, such as course numbers and course icons.

A course number, for instance, can be useful in sorting report and search results in some systems. It is sometimes helpful to create a convention that embeds keys to the nature of the course within the course number.

For example, in Table 10-1, a basic classroom course offered in French by the sales and marketing organization in Canada titled Introduction to Solution Selling would be assigned the course number SM.ISS.101cnf:

- *SM* represents the department sponsoring the course: sales and marketing.
- *ISS* represents the initials of the title, Introduction to Solution Selling.
- *101* indicates that it is a basic level course.
- *c* indicates that the format is classroom.
- *n* indicates that the course is offered in the North America region.
- *f* indicates that the course is delivered in the French language.

Table 10-1. Course Numbering Convention Example

2 chars	*n* chars	3 nums	1 char	1 char	1 char
fa Finance and Accounting	First letter of each word in course title	101 Basic	b Blended	a Asia, Pacific Rim	First letter of language name
hr Human Resources		201 Intermediate	c Classroom	e Europe, Middle East, Africa	
it Information Technology		301 Advanced	e E-Learning	g Global	
pm Product Management			v Virtual Class	n North America	
sm Sales and Marketing				s Central America, South America, Caribbean	

Some organizations go a step further than the course number to design a collection of icons whose symbols and colors indicate to users, at a glance, a course's delivery mode, whether it is free or has a cost associated with it, and other course properties. While these types of conventions are not necessary, they can add valuable cues that save people time and effort as they use the LMS.

Consistent Use of Course Properties

Every LMS contains a set of configurable course properties. Some course properties, such as title and description, are consistent for all types of courses. Other course properties vary based on the type of course. For example, an online course has a launch method and URL, while an instructor-led course has an instructor, location, start date and time, and end date and time.

When considering your organization's needs, you may decide to standardize some course property settings. Let's say you charge a registration fee for a course. People who withdraw from the course at the last minute cause you to lose money that has already been spent to reserve a classroom, hire an instructor, and furnish course materials. In this case, you might want to establish a cutoff date for withdrawing from the course. People who withdraw before the cutoff date receive a full refund. People who withdraw after the cutoff date receive only a partial refund, or no refund at all.

It's important to document these standards and communicate them to LMS administrators. Adherence to these standards will ensure consistency in how courses are configured in the system, which will improve your reports and make the system easier to administer. Standards do not need to be communicated to users explicitly. They will simply make the LMS easy to understand and use.

Consistent Use of Course Structures

Many LMS products offer a variety of modules or learning activity types that can be assembled in different combinations. Administrators use these modules to create courses in the system.

Course structures may contain various activities like classes, self-paced modules, and surveys. Activities may be arranged in an enforced sequence or at the user's option. A higher-level curriculum or learning path structure may contain several courses, each containing its own learning activities.

For example, Course A may consist of a webinar followed by a test and survey. An administrator would assemble the course structure for Course A using a webinar module, test module, and survey module. The administrator may configure the course structure so that the survey cannot be started until the test is completed and the test cannot be started until the webinar has taken place.

Course B may consist of three online, self-paced courses and a survey. An administrator would assemble the course structure for Course B using three online modules and a survey module. The administrator may configure this course structure so that the three online modules can be taken in any order, but all three must be completed before the survey can be accessed.

Because many LMS products offer a variety of ways to accomplish the same result, it is important that you define, document, and communicate standards for how your organization's learning programs should be structured. When courses of a similar nature are structured consistently, learners taking those courses become more familiar with how to access and complete them.

Communicating and Enforcing Standards

Once you have established all your standards, it is important to communicate them through administrator training, job aids, and guides.

I have seen organizations enforce their standards in a variety of ways. Some organizations assign a super-administrator, who spot-checks the work of other administrators to ensure they are applying the standards appropriately. When problems are found, the super-administrator provides coaching and follows up with more frequent spot-checks until the issue is resolved. Other organizations train their LMS administrators and then get them started with extra supervision and mentoring until they demonstrate that they can perform all their responsibilities and apply the standards appropriately. At that point, they become "certified" and no longer require supervision. Certified administrators later become mentors to new administrators, and the cycle continues.

Every organization is different, but all should establish, communicate, and enforce standards.

Taxonomy

It's been said that we spend anywhere between 15 and 35 percent of our time searching for content (Feldman 2004), and that was in the early days of the Internet, when the amount of available information was smaller by several magnitudes of order. The better you organize and tag content, the easier it is to find. In the LMS, courses are organized in several ways. Administrators will place courses in your catalog menu structure, tag them with metadata, and associate them with audiences that have been defined from profile data. Together, these features make up your LMS taxonomy.

There may be several instances throughout the lifetime of your LMS when you need to update the taxonomy to reflect changes in your subject matter and learning program offerings.

Taxonomy Design

When designing your taxonomy, it is important to design through the eyes of those who will use the catalog to find courses and consider how the course is tagged with metadata to evaluate whether the courses they have found meet their needs. Try to maintain a consistent level of detail in your taxonomy design so that items in your catalog menus are categorically similar. Avoid ambiguity by ensuring that metadata items are distinct so that administrators will know how to tag content. Balance hierarchical structures so that menus are kept to a reasonable number of items and can be taken in at a glance. Table 10-2 shows good and poor examples of course catalog menus.

Usability Testing

Chapter 9 described the LMS implementation process of user acceptance testing. That process was about checking the system's functionality to make sure it was working properly and ready to go live. Although usability testing may sound like a similar process, it is very different. Usability testing is focused on determining how easy the system is for people to use. It answers the questions: Can people navigate the system intuitively? Is there a clear path to action? And can people accomplish what they are trying to do quickly and directly?

Table 10-2. Examples of Course Catalog Menus

Good Example	Poor Example
• Corporate Orientation Programs ■ Diversity ■ Ethics ■ Health and Safety ■ New Employee Orientation ■ New Manager Orientation • Functional Skill Development ■ Communications ■ Finance ■ Information Technology ■ Legal ■ Marketing and Sales ■ Quality • Leadership Skill Development ■ Decision Making ■ Delegating ■ Developing Others ■ Listening Skills ■ Motivating and Influencing Others ■ Problem Solving ■ Teamwork • Products and Services Training ■ Product X ■ Product Y ■ Service Z	• Accounting ■ Bookkeeping ■ Finance ■ General Ledger • Contracts • Leadership Skills ■ Decision Making ■ Delegating ■ Finance ■ Motivating and Influencing Others • Management Skills ■ Decision Making ■ Delegating ■ Developing Others ■ Diversity ■ Ethics ■ Teamwork • New Employee Orientation • New Manager Orientation • Product X • Product Y • Quality ■ Health and Safety ■ Quality • Sales Skills • Service Z • Vouchers

Foreman (2013e).

It's always good to test your taxonomy's usability with learners and administrators, especially if you have little experience with creating taxonomies. Testing is easy to do, doesn't take long, and provides valuable feedback that you can use to tweak your taxonomy before you implement it.

To do this, establish five to seven goals for the test subject to attempt by using the taxonomy. An example of a goal is, "Find a course that can help you manage your time." Invite three to five people, who are representative of your end users, to participate as test subjects.

Conduct the test with each person, individually. Ask each test subject to attempt to accomplish the goals you have identified. Do not interfere. If the subject hesitates or gets stuck, ask them to verbalize their thoughts. Observe, take notes, or make a video recording of the test.

Once the usability test has been completed with all test subjects, review your notes and recordings. List the findings from all test subjects. Analyze the findings and use them to refine your taxonomy. Repeat the usability test if needed. An iterative approach to taxonomy design and testing can yield great results.

Implementing the Taxonomy

Once you have finalized your taxonomy design, you will need to implement it in your LMS. For a new implementation, this is just a matter of configuring the system. If you are changing the taxonomy of a live system, you will need to proceed carefully.

First, configure the taxonomy in a staging server environment—that is, an installation of your LMS that is not accessible to end users but mirrors your production (user-facing) system. Document the steps you take to implement the taxonomy in the staging environment so that you can repeat the same steps later, in production.

Devise an implementation plan that minimizes disruption to your end users. Engage administrators and content owners to assist in retagging content with the new metadata and moving courses to the right location in the new catalog structure. Work with your IT organization and LMS vendor to explore whether part or all of the transition to the new taxonomy can be automated and performed during off-peak hours. Communicate the change to your users to set expectations around the period of potential disruption, and assure them of the new taxonomy's ultimate benefits. If you have done usability testing, you can communicate the customer-focused message that users were involved in designing the new taxonomy.

Configuration Management

I have worked with many organizations in which no one really knows how the LMS is configured or whether it is working properly. The people who made the original configuration decisions are long gone and did not leave any documentation. But then tags break, courses disappear from the catalog, credits are not issued properly, reports stop working, or any number of other things that can go wrong happen. And no one knows how to fix them.

> **Ask This**
>
> Work with your IT organization and LMS vendor to see if transition to the new taxonomy can be automated and performed during off-peak hours.

Note the same is true for systems integrations. Since the LMS was first integrated, your organization may have updated or changed the LMS configuration or that of another system. These changes may cause working parts to break. Resulting data problems may go undetected.

For this reason, it is important to document your configuration decisions and keep the documentation up-to-date whenever changes are made. The LMS configuration settings you should document include, at a minimum, access and authentication, data feeds, user account and profile settings, security roles and permissions, audience rules, catalog and metadata taxonomies, transcripts and certificates, active notifications, and look and feel settings. Maintaining LMS configuration documentation enables you to plan and make changes to the configuration more easily, understand the impact of the changes on other settings, and provide clear direction to your vendor or IT department. You may want to consult your vendor or IT department for a template or guidance on how to best document your configuration. I use a variety of text document or spreadsheet formats, based on the LMS product, client configuration, or client IT standards.

Housekeeping

When your workspace becomes messy and things are not in their proper place, you have difficulty finding what you need when you need it. The same thing happens in your LMS. Over time, some of your courses may be tagged or placed in the catalog improperly, administrators may have deviated from standards, duplicate user accounts may exist along with accounts for people who left the organization long ago, and so on. These and other problems will eventually make your data unreliable.

The best time to clean up your data is when you migrate to a new LMS product or perform a major upgrade to an existing LMS. At these times, it is less challenging to identify cleanup requirements and tasks and build them into your project plan, leveraging the resources that are already assigned to the implementation.

If you cannot take advantage of a system upgrade or migration, you can still clean up your data. But you may need to establish the LMS cleanup as a formal project to assign the necessary resources, time, and effort to make it happen.

In either case, your main goal is to bring your LMS data up to the standards your organization has defined. Here are the steps you should take:

1. Create an inventory of the data that need to be purged or cleaned up:
    - » Consider your organization's data retention policy.
    - » Identify courses that should be archived.
    - » Identify user accounts to be deactivated and duplicate accounts to be merged.
    - » Determine how much historic data must be saved and what can be purged from the system.
2. Make a comprehensive list of any configuration changes you intend to make and determine how data will be affected.
3. Carefully plot out the cleanup process:
    - » Define all steps. Assign who is responsible for each step.
    - » Identify the steps that can be done on the current system before the migration or upgrade and those that must happen afterward. Check and double-check your plan to ensure that nothing has been missed.
    - » If you anticipate a need to take the production system offline to perform some of the steps, carefully plan what must be done, when it will be done, who will do it, and how you will know it has been done accurately to minimize system downtime.
    - » Automate as much of the cleanup process as possible by working with your IT department or LMS vendor to create database scripts that can be run to clean up the data based on rules and parameters you have defined.
4. Before you perform the actual cleanup tasks on the production system, practice the process from start to finish:

   - Ask your IT department or LMS vendor to copy the production system to a staging server environment, which is inaccessible to users.
   - Rehearse the process on the staging server.
   - Document any changes or additions to the steps in the plan based on the results of your rehearsal.
   - If necessary, ask IT or your vendor to reset the staging environment and repeat the rehearsal until you are satisfied it can be conducted effectively and expeditiously in the production environment.
5. When you are ready to perform the cleanup process in your production environment:
   - Ask IT or your LMS vendor to back up the production database.
   - Perform the cleanup tasks that can be done while the server is online.
   - Notify end users of the system outage, bring the system down, and perform the offline cleanup tasks.
   - Bring the system back up and perform any additional cleanup activities in the live system.
   - Thoroughly test the system configuration to validate that your cleanup has been completed effectively and that no new, unforeseen problems have emerged.

Governance

System governance ensures that the LMS implementation aligns with the goals and needs of the organization. Governance establishes appropriate representation from all stakeholder groups and provides a structure for decision making. Without adequate governance, you may not have the authority to establish and enforce standards.

While each organization may establish its own unique governance structure, there is a basic governance model that can be helpful. The groups within this structure interact to ensure that LMS issues are managed at the appropriate level and any unresolved or systemic issues are escalated. Figure 10-2 depicts a sample governance structure comprising four main parts: a governing board representing executive leadership, an LMS steering team representing management, LMS working groups that represent key stakeholders who use the LMS directly, and LMS operations.

Figure 10-2. Sample Governance Structure

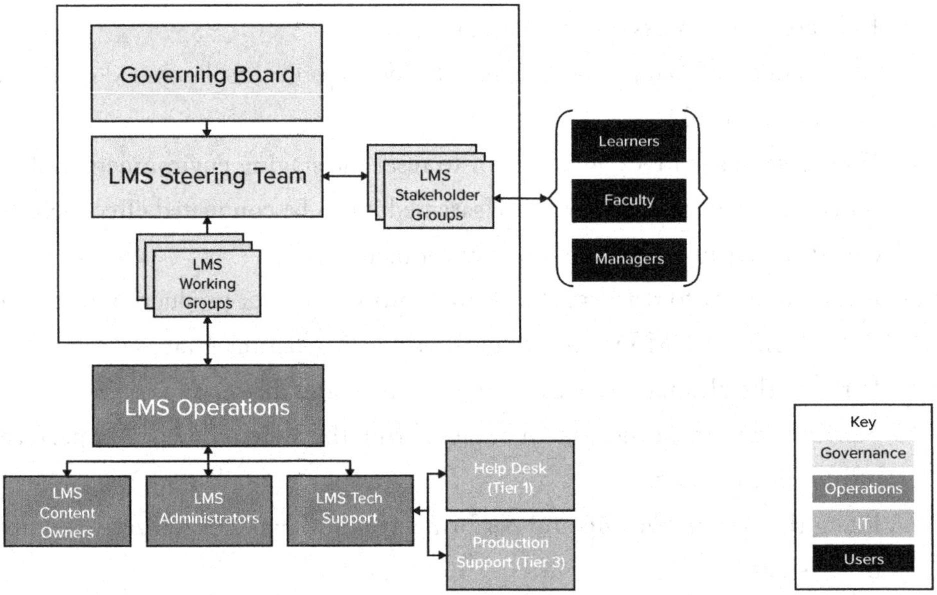

Governing Board

A governing board consists of key stakeholders at the executive leadership level. The board represents the organization's strategic goals. The governing board is not focused on technology behind the LMS. Its mission is to provide direction to ensure linkage between organizational strategy and learning strategy. The governing board may convene one or two times per year.

LMS Steering Team

The LMS steering team consists of key stakeholders at the management level. Each team member represents one or more user groups that rely on the LMS. This could include learners, managers, and faculty in different functional areas or departments. The LMS steering team's mission is to establish learning management practices and policies. The team may convene quarterly.

LMS Working Groups

LMS working groups consist of key stakeholders who use the LMS directly. Each group represents a special area of focus, such as taxonomy or standards. The mission of the working groups is to plan and execute activities related to LMS usability and operations. Groups may convene six times a year, and more often during special initiatives.

LMS Operations

The LMS operations structure itself typically consists of four groups: the group that manages LMS operations, content owners, administrators, and technical support.

LMS Operations Management

The LMS operations management team is responsible for ensuring that the LMS operates reliably, is managed in conformance with standards, and meets the needs of the organization. The operations management team works closely with the working groups and steering team, helping to surface issues that need attention.

Content Owners

LMS content owners are responsible for the quality of the learning programs they own—that is, their accuracy, relevance, and timeliness. Content owners must provide appropriate information about the learning program to enable LMS administrators to configure the learning program based on the LMS standards. Content owners must be vigilant in monitoring utilization by the learning program's target audience and ensuring that the program is kept up-to-date.

LMS Administrators

LMS administrators are responsible for the accuracy and thoroughness of the way in which content is configured in the LMS. They must provide a timely response to requests from content owners. LMS administrators must consistently implement LMS standards, conventions, policies, and processes.

Technical Support

LMS technical support may consist of some combination of training, IT, and vendor staff. Technical support groups may include your help desk, e-learning content developers, developers of custom reports, server support, database and application managers, IT security, and network support. Together, these technical support groups are responsible for keeping the LMS up and running, resolving end-user issues, ensuring that any web-based programs work properly, developing custom reports, managing any changes to the system configuration, and installing patches and updates.

* * *

Although it would be nice, it is extremely unlikely that you can simply buy an LMS, install it, and just let it do its thing. Remember, it's not just about acquiring the technology; it's also about how well the technology is *used.* LMS implementation can be challenging, but the payoff is huge. Taking steps to establish and maintain standards, taxonomy, configuration management, housekeeping, and governance will help ensure that your LMS remains easy to use and operate for years to come.

Key Takeaways

This chapter focused on how to get the most from your LMS with effective standards, taxonomy, housekeeping, configuration management, and governance. The key takeaways are:

- Standards are a critical ingredient in making an LMS easy to use and administer, yet too many organizations operate without them.
- At a minimum, you need four key policies: content inclusion, content ownership, content life-cycle management, and training data retention.
- Clearly documented and communicated administrative procedures help ensure that learning is managed in a methodical way, consistent with the standards and policies.
- Guidelines and conventions for course titles and course numbers make it easier for people to find relevant content, by avoiding inconsistency, redundancy, and ambiguity.
- With multiple administrators, a common set of standards for configuring learning programs makes the LMS easier to use.
- The LMS taxonomy organizes the content and includes the course catalog menu structure, course metadata tags that enhance searching and reporting, and user profile data used to create course audiences.
- It is important to document your current LMS configuration, along with reasons for your configuration decisions, and keep it up-to-date to inform future changes.

- Implementing a major LMS upgrade or new LMS presents opportunities to clean up your data.
- Governance is critical to your ongoing LMS operations. There is a general model for a governance structure that you can use as a starting point in establishing your own.

This concludes part 2 of the book, which was focused on LMS implementation and operation. Part 3 explores future trends and the role of the LMS in a broader learning and performance ecosystem.

PART 3

Beyond the LMS

CHAPTER 11

LMS Trends: Current and Future

This chapter explains how the LMS is gradually transitioning from the core L&D technology to being one system among many that support learning.

The LMS became firmly established as a product category in the late 1990s. Since that time, there seems to be a doomsday prophesy every few years from people in the L&D field who believe that the end of the LMS is near. The most prevalent argument is that the LMS is limited, for the most part, to delivering courses. Today, we recognize that people learn not just from courses, but through social media, performance support, adaptive simulations, instructional games, short videos, and many other methods that do not adhere to the course registration and completion model that is rigidly enforced by the LMS.

So, is the end of the LMS at hand? The answer is clearly no. The LMS marketplace is still evolving, with new products emerging all the time. As you read this, there are hundreds of organizations considering, evaluating, purchasing, or implementing an LMS. Some of them are ready for their first LMS; others are on their fourth or fifth.

As long as organizations need to deliver courses, they will need an LMS. Training will always be a useful approach to meeting regulatory compliance requirements, orienting people to a new job, and helping people get to baseline competence. Many learning and development groups have a well-oiled machine for developing and delivering courses. So, courses and the LMS products that manage them are not going away any time soon.

Still, the LMS industry has, for the most part, sidestepped the problem of how to support learning and performance solutions that are not packaged as courses. Back in 2003, Stephen Segrave and Dale Holt pointed out in their article on how universities are adopting technology-based learning solutions, "The LMS may not, on its own, be sufficiently conducive to supporting the design, development and operations required within contemporary learning environments." As the use of noncourse solutions grows, the LMS will gradually lose its position as learning and development's core technology—the one-stop shop where people find everything available to help them learn and develop—and, instead, become simply one of many systems that support learning.

The LMS as One System Among Many

As the variety of solutions that support learning and performance grows, the LMS is gradually starting to move away from the center of an organization's learning technology infrastructure and becoming one of many special purpose learning technologies. Many organizations are beginning to treat the LMS as a special purpose technology for delivering and tracking structured learning programs. But to support learning that happens outside courses, organizations are turning to other technologies. These include social networking and collaboration tools, performance support systems, searchable knowledge bases, expert networks, instructional games and simulations, augmented reality solutions, and adaptive learning platforms. Learning and development organizations are adding these systems, on their own or in collaboration with IT and HR, to enhance the learning technology infrastructure. Together, these systems provide a powerful tool set that enables you to go beyond course delivery to support performance in the workplace and establish online environments where people can learn on their own or from one another.

All the systems used by learning and development, and the content within them, can be connected in a variety of ways. You can work with your IT department to tie these systems together through the use of single sign-on, deep linking to content between systems, enterprise search across systems, and a learning record store to collect data from multiple systems.

Chapter 5 described the ADL's total learning architecture initiative, more evidence that organizations are moving beyond the LMS and making use of a broader set of tools to provide advanced learning and performance solutions. Look for the transformation of the LMS from the main system for learning and development, to one system among many. The next chapter on learning and performance ecosystems goes deeper on this topic.

The LMS as a Transcript Warehouse

As learning professionals expand their learning and development solutions beyond courses, they will still need to record people's learning. Using mechanisms like xAPI, you can track as much information as you like about how people are using the various pieces of a learning and performance solution, even those that occur outside the LMS.

One of my clients recently developed a blended learning program that involved assignments, research using a knowledge base, and participation in a community of practice. The program did not live on the LMS. Instead, it was delivered directly to employees through a portal, knowledge management system, and social network. They used xAPI to track people's activities across all these platforms and recorded the data in a learning record store. They created a simple course shell—course title, course number, and course credit hours, but no content—in the LMS just to record completions. The course shell was hidden from the LMS catalog and people did not register through the LMS. The LRS and LMS were integrated so that when a specific number and combination of milestones was reached in the LRS, a completion was recorded automatically in the LMS and credit was added to the person's transcript.

In this way, the organization used the LMS to record achievements, issue credit, and maintain transcripts for learning and performance solutions supported by learning technologies and content repositories that were separate from the LMS.

This example, and others, reinforces how learning programs are beginning to escape the boundaries of the LMS, even while organizations and learning professionals continue to use the LMS to issue credit and provide the official transcript.

Unwrapping the LMS

For years, experts have been saying the LMS will no longer be a monolithic system with its own web address where people go to fulfill their training needs. Instead, it will be "unwrapped" so that its internal parts can be made available to other websites and applications. Essentially, the LMS will change from a system into a plug-in capability. The learning management plug-in will provide a course repository and a library of learning management functions that can be built directly into workplace systems, portals, and websites. While not widespread yet, this change is happening in two ways.

First, organizations are using LMS application programming interfaces to pull out the course descriptions and post them on websites and portals. A mouse click triggers the LMS registration API. In a sense, these organizations are replacing the LMS user interface with their own website, where the content and functionality can be mixed seamlessly with other information.

Second, more LMS products are becoming available not just as stand-alone systems but as apps and plug-ins that run within web development frameworks like WordPress, Salesforce, and SharePoint. So organizations that use one of these products can add LMS functionality directly and seamlessly into their site, without the need to develop a custom integration. This is particularly useful if your organization sells courses, or if it provides courses that train people to use the products you sell. The courses can be linked into your web shopping site, where the courses can be linked to your products, or be products on their own.

In these ways, the LMS becomes ubiquitous as an integral part of your organization's broader web presence.

Gamifying the LMS

Competition can be motivating. Points, badges, and leaderboards will become more prevalent in the LMS. I have worked with several retail organizations that have franchised stores and use a gamified LMS approach to feed healthy competition between stores. They use leaderboards to show which stores have earned the most points and badges related to the store employees' achievement of learning goals. A gamified LMS can add a fun dimension to what may otherwise be perceived as dull and boring learning programs.

For several years, the larger course development vendors have offered gamified LMS platforms custom developed to deliver their own gamified e-learning programs. Now, the Open Badge Infrastructure specification makes it possible for commercial LMS manufacturers to build gamification into their systems in a standardized way that will work with most commercial authoring tools.

Advanced Ways to Connect People With Content

Many of the most useful website features to which we have become accustomed were first introduced on retail sites. For example, the shopping cart and checkout experience found in many LMS products are all based on retail website models. LMS companies will begin to incorporate other retail features that help connect people with relevant content.

What if an LMS could automatically recognize affinities between ourselves and other users and recommend content used by other people like us, perhaps saying, "People who completed this course also took . . ." or "People in your job role took . . ."?

Or it could provide personalized recommendations based on predictive analytics: "Based on other courses you've taken, you may be interested in. . . ."

These types of features could add value to LMS products by providing another way for people to find relevant content. As the LMS marketplace continues to evolve and become increasingly competitive, look for more LMS innovations that mimic tried-and-true practices on retail sites.

The LMS and Talent Management

Many LMS providers have expanded into a broader set of HR functions, commonly referred to as talent management. These talent management systems provide support for recruiting and hiring, performance management, succession planning, career development, workforce planning, and more. In many of these systems, competencies are the glue that binds people who have or need competencies, jobs that require competencies, and training that helps develop competencies.

In recruitment and hiring, jobs can be associated with the competencies required to do the job well. These competencies are then targeted in recruitment and candidate assessment.

In performance management, the professional development plans of incumbents are focused on addressing competency gaps through courses mapped to those competencies in the LMS.

In succession planning, high-potential leadership candidates can be identified and development plans can be crafted to grow their leadership competencies. Leadership development plans may include courses in the LMS.

In career development, employees can select a target job and compare their own self-assessed competencies with those required for the new job. These employees can then create personalized career development plans to develop needed skills to prepare for their desired positions. Their development plans may include courses in the LMS, relevant to their competency gaps.

In workforce planning, business objectives are established and workforce competencies needed to achieve the objectives are identified. The talent management system provides data on the readiness of the workforce and helps leaders make decisions on staff assignments, such as whether to rely on the current skill set of its employees, upskill existing people, hire new people, or outsource. If upskilling is needed, relevant courses are identified or added to the LMS.

Getting Better at What an LMS Does Well

LMS companies are continually enhancing their products in response to changes in technology, requests from customers, and innovations introduced by competitors. Here are some key areas to look for LMS improvements.

cmi5 Support

Look for LMS products to support cmi5, which does what SCORM did but much better (see chapter 5 for more information). It uses newer web technologies, does not generate SCORM pop-ups that cause problems with users' pop-up blockers, and will work for people who want to access courses using mobile devices, unlike SCORM.

Mobile Users

Look for LMS products to provide better support for mobile users. Some LMS products still use pop-up menus, mouse-over prompts, and other features that do not translate well for mobile users. Some products continue to require a lot of vertical and horizontal scrolling on smaller screens. Look for these "laggers" to follow the lead of some of the more forward-looking LMS products. The progressive ones are well designed for access through a browser using any device, or they offer an app that provides a simplified user experience using accordion controls and other interface methods that work well on a touch device.

Streamlined Administrator Experience

One of the complaints I hear most frequently from LMS administrators is the fact that course and event data entry is too cumbersome. LMS products must balance the flexibility of feature-rich administrator tools with the simplicity of reducing repetitive tasks and streamlining administrator processes. Some products do not go far enough in making the product easy to understand. Look for LMS products to become easier for administrators to use.

Search

There are many powerful search technologies available, yet most LMS products fail to take advantage of them. Instead, they use native database search tools that lack features like spell checkers, "did you mean . . ." functionality, finding all forms of a word, and results ranked by relevance.

Think about how your favorite web search tool works. If you spell a word incorrectly, it often gives you the right results as if your spelling were correct. When you enter a word or acronym that is similar to what you want, but not quite right, the search tool will prompt you with, "Did you mean . . .?" and a list of one or more closely related terms. Searching on a word like *writing* returns results related to *writing, writer,* and *writers.* Most of the time, you are likely to find the result you want on the first page of the search results, often in the first three items listed.

That's not how search works for LMS products. You will only see the results you are seeking if you search *exactly* on what you seek, spell it correctly, and use the exact form of the word; even then, you may have to search through pages of results to find what you want. Look for LMS products to replace blunt database search functionality with more feature-rich search capabilities that resemble the Internet search tools to which we've all become accustomed.

Reports

LMS reports are already becoming more graphical. More LMS products will offer customizable dashboards where administrators and learners can select libraries of data widgets to create personalized views of the information the LMS tracks. The widgets will display data in pie charts, bar charts, cluster charts, heat maps, and other graphical ways, making the data easier to visualize. Of course, you will still be able to click on a graphic and drill down to more detailed textual reports.

More Features at Lower Cost

The cost of LMS products is dropping thanks to newer, less expensive approaches to software development, the fact that the LMS feature set is clearly defined, and healthy competition in the marketplace. With the introduction of new products by smaller, hungrier companies, LMS customers have more options every year. Many LMS companies offer flexible and negotiable licensing terms. An increasing number of high-quality open source products are available with no licensing fees at all. Look for low-cost LMS products to become more feature-rich, and high-cost products to get cheaper.

Related Learning Systems

There are a few more types of systems that should be mentioned because they are closely related to the LMS: MOOC (massive open online course) delivery systems, online program management, and microlearning delivery systems.

MOOC Delivery Systems

Massive open online courses are not new; they were first introduced in 2006 and are now an established niche in the academic world. You can find these courses on the web, and most can be taken free of charge, although some providers offer additional fee-based personalized services and completion certificates.

There are several commercial and open source products used to deliver MOOCs. In 2012, Harvard and MIT partnered to develop a platform called Open EdX, which is available free for use by other academic institutions.

While MOOCs aren't learning management systems, they offer some overlapping features for administering and accessing learning content and supporting learner and instructor interactions.

Online Program Management

Many colleges and universities continue to expand beyond the campus to reach students through online continuing education and degree programs. Yet, some institutions lack the resources to establish the technology infrastructure and operations to support online education. Several education software and publishing companies offer online program management services that essentially outsource the technology and operations for delivering online education.

Microlearning Delivery Systems

Microlearning is a growing trend in the business world. It happens through quick tutorials, explanations, demonstrations, and walk-throughs. It often takes the form of short instructional and informational videos.

There are a growing number of products that specialize in delivering microlearning. Some of these products also provide social features for blogs, user ratings, posting, and replying to comments on content and topics. These microlearning delivery systems have some features similar to an LMS but specialize in the microlearning format.

Key Takeaways

This chapter explored current and future LMS trends. The key takeaways are:

- Look for the LMS to move from the most important L&D technology to being one system among many.
- Look for the LMS to update learner transcripts and issue credits for learning that happens outside the LMS, functioning as a transcript warehouse.
- Look for the LMS to become increasingly "unwrapped" so that its content and functionality can be plugged into existing portals and websites.
- Look for more commercial LMS products to introduce gamification features such as points, badges, and leaderboards.
- Look for the LMS to get much better at what it already does pretty well, shifting from SCORM to cmi5, offering better mobile user interfaces, becoming more streamlined and easier for administrators to use, and offering enhanced search capabilities and personalized dashboards.
- While its feature set grows, the price of the LMS will drop as more open source and low-cost products continue to enter the market.
- There are two types of systems related to the LMS: MOOC delivery systems and microlearning delivery systems.

The next chapter explores the LMS's role in the broader learning and performance ecosystem.

CHAPTER 12

The LMS's Role in the Learning and Performance Ecosystem

This chapter introduces the concept of a learning and performance ecosystem that supports not just courses, but all the ways people learn.

Think about the last time you had to figure out how to do something new. For many people, it's a weekly or daily occurrence. Now think about how many of those times you got it done by first taking a course. The answer is probably not often. So how did you manage to do it?

As shown in Figure 12-1, training is only one of the ways people learn how to do things. Taking courses can be an effective way to get to baseline proficiency, but you cannot expect to become an expert through training alone. People progress toward mastery in their education and personal and professional lives through practicing and gaining experience, using tools and resources, exploring information, observing and networking with others, consulting with experts, and other ways. Most of these are experiential, meaning that learning occurs in the context of getting things done in the real world.

Figure 12-1. Ways People Learn

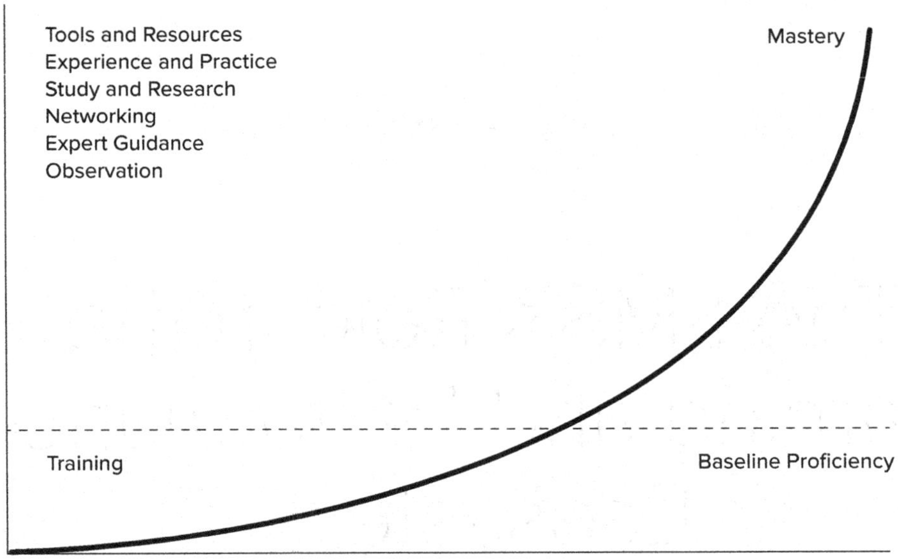

Adapted from Foreman (2010) and Rosenberg and Foreman (2014).

In his book, *Deep Learning Manual,* Arthur J. Murray (2015) asserts that many typical courses lack context and practical application and therefore result in little more than surface learning. His premise is that people often learn more effectively through their own research, exploration, and discovery.

In academic settings, experiential learning is being driven, in part, by research in the effectiveness of evidence- and inquiry-based teaching practices. In their book, *A New Culture of Learning,* authors Douglas Thomas and John Seely Brown (2011) explain how successful institutions of higher education are doing much more than transferring knowledge in the classroom. They are developing students experientially through immersive projects, mentoring, and internships with a focus on helping students learn how to use information and technology for continued self-development.

In a business setting, experiential learning may not involve teaching at all. In *Beyond E-Learning,* author Marc Rosenberg (2006) states that a company's ultimate goal is to "make learning and work so indistinguishable from one another, so mutually beneficial, that learning becomes work and work becomes learning."

The Role of L&D

What does all of this mean to the L&D professional? Despite a widespread name change from *training* to *learning and development,* many L&D departments have been unable to transcend their traditional role: that they exist to create and deliver courses. And this is not just how L&D is perceived by the rest of the organization; many L&D departments view themselves the same way. As long as L&D departments continue to limit their products and services to courses and teaching, their potential impact is diminished.

Here's a story that may sound familiar to you, either in your own organization or in one you've heard about. I once worked with an L&D department that measured its own success based on how many people took its courses. It opened a world-class training facility. To attract students, it transformed its cafeteria into a restaurant with a waitstaff and offered free mobile devices to people who attended courses. Enrollments skyrocketed for a time, but when the economy slowed, the department's funding was cut to almost nothing and its training center was shut down. L&D's metrics proved it had delivered lots of courses to lots of employees, and data showed that people liked the courses and the pass rate was very high, so they were clearly satisfied and learning something. But the department could provide no evidence of its true value to the business. Don't let this happen to your organization. The ideal position for the L&D function is to be viewed as an essential partner in helping the organization succeed. Training is important, for sure, but you will never generate real and sustainable value if all you do is training.

Think about your L&D department's mission. Is it to deliver training? That is an activity rather than an outcome. Is it to ensure that people learn? That is an outcome, but it may influence you to operate more like a school than a business function. Consider all the L&D organizations that refer to themselves as a school or corporate university. If your department is focused on improving job performance, it's probably doing a better job at supporting the business.

The goal of executive leadership—those who fund L&D—is to improve employee productivity as a significant contributor to the bottom line. Don't be surprised if your sponsors react negatively to boasts about the large numbers of people taking your courses. After all, the productivity of someone taking a course is zero. Executive leadership does not care whether people take the courses, like the courses, pass the tests, or change behavior when back on the job. While those metrics can be helpful within L&D, they are meaningless in the larger business context. The metrics your funders care about are related to productivity and business results.

Today, L&D is at a crossroads. The old road leads to more of the same, in which L&D continues to operate as a training department. The new road leads to a reinvention of L&D, in which it broadens its solution set, becomes a strategic partner to its sponsors, and has a more direct and measurable impact on business success. An increasing number of L&D organizations are beginning to travel this new road by actively working to build new capabilities and offer a broader suite of products and services.

An emerging way to look at the broader L&D role is to consider an entire "ecosystem" of tools and approaches that support learning and performance. Your courses and the LMS that delivers them are still important, but they no longer take center stage. A learning and performance ecosystem allows you to conceive, create, and deliver a broader suite of L&D products.

What Is a Learning and Performance Ecosystem?

A learning and performance ecosystem puts people in the center and supports them with six primary components: talent management, performance support, knowledge management, access to experts, social networking and collaboration, and structured learning. From these six components, you can create any number of dynamic learning and performance solutions. Figure 12-2 showcases the ecosystem and reveals many different combinations of solutions that can help people learn more, learn faster, and perform their jobs better. Several of these components enable you to embed experiential learning in the workflow.

The learning and performance ecosystem provides a framework for gaining synergy from all the learning tools and models at your disposal. Organizations adopting the ecosystem framework recognize that training is not the only way to improve performance. People also develop and become more productive through opportunities to advance, perform, research, consult, and share.

In Table 12-1, you can see the major differences between a focus solely on training and learning, and a broader focus on a learning and performance ecosystem. The training or learning function does not disappear; it's just subsumed under the much bigger ecosystem paradigm.

Figure 12-2. Learning and Performance Ecosystem

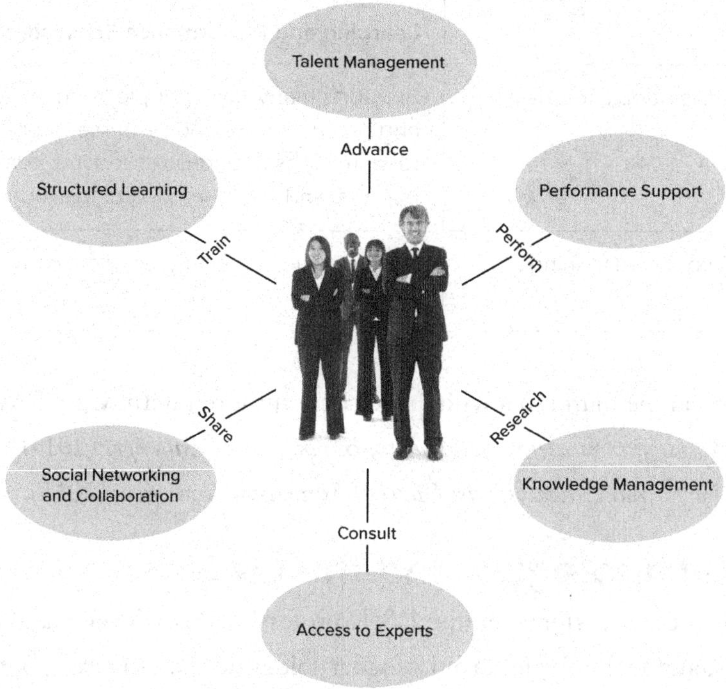

Adapted from Foreman (2010) and Rosenberg and Foreman (2014).

Table 12-1. Paradigm Shift From Training to the Learning and Performance Ecosystem

Training	**Learning and Performance Ecosystem**
Focuses on what people need to know.	Focuses on what people need to be able to do.
Tends to put content in the center.	Always puts the performer in the center.
People interrupt their work to take training.	Workflow is interrupted only as a last resort. More often, people learn and get support while working.
Often linear and static. Front-end analysis leads to course development, which leads to course delivery.	Always adaptable. An ongoing practice of continuous analysis and solution refinement sustains the ecosystem solution, helping it adapt and thrive.

Table 12-1. Paradigm Shift From Training to the Learning and Performance Ecosystem (cont.)

Training	Learning and Performance Ecosystem
Supports one of the ways people learn—taking courses.	Supports many ways people learn: experience and practice, tools and resources, self-study and research, observation, networking, consulting with experts, and structured learning programs.
Evaluation focuses on your own training metrics.	Evaluation focuses on your sponsor's productivity metrics.

More information can be found in a whitepaper I co-authored with Marc Rosenberg, *Learning and Performance Ecosystems: Strategy, Technology, Impact, and Challenges* (2014) and my research report, *Learning and Performance Ecosystems: Current State and Challenges* (2015).

Ecosystem Technologies and the LMS

Learning and performance ecosystems require L&D professionals to develop and apply a broader set of skills, processes, and technologies. Your broader role is not just to teach, but to create environments where people can learn on their own, and from one another. A large part of your job is to enable connectedness by introducing people to job-relevant tools, information, and other people.

So how does learning management fit into the learning and performance ecosystem? While an LMS is very good at managing the delivery of structured learning programs, it is not a very effective knowledge base or performance support system. The LMS is one important ingredient, but a learning and performance ecosystem must also incorporate other learning technologies that support social networking, knowledge bases, interaction with experts, performance support, and talent management.

Your IT and HR departments may have already deployed some of these technologies. As you design your learning and performance solutions, look beyond the LMS for opportunities to leverage the applications your IT and HR partners have already deployed. Scan the learning technologies marketplace for other products that can help you build a more advanced tool set. Much of the system selection, implementation, and operation guidance in this book can be applied to other technology projects as you continue to expand your learning technology tool set.

How do you measure learning that happens outside the LMS? Consider using xAPI to track learning activities that take place on all your different technology platforms. You can find out more about the xAPI in a research report I co-authored with ADL experts Peter Berking, Jason Haag, and Craig Wiggins, *The Experience API: Liberating Learning Design* (2014).

Preparing for Success With Your LMS Initiative

While the LMS may not be the central, most important technology supporting your learning and development strategy, it is still a critical component. LMS products have become very sophisticated over the years. They can support many divergent ways in which different organizations manage course delivery, and they will continue to expand and improve in the coming years.

Now that we've discussed how to select, implement, and operate an LMS, you are ready for your own LMS initiative. I have observed that the average life span of an LMS implementation is about five years. If that is true, your organization may go through the evaluation, selection, and implementation process twice every decade. In your career, you are likely to be involved directly, or at least peripherally, in an LMS implementation at least once or twice. You and your team must be ready for this large-scale project.

LMS projects can be daunting, and there will surely be challenges along the way. You may face pressure to acquire the technology despite unrealistic funding expectations, in the midst of organizational change, or in the absence of a clear learning strategy. You might encounter resistance and conflicting priorities from key stakeholders. Gaining the trust, support, and cooperation of your IT department may be challenging. At times, members of your LMS project team will have different viewpoints on how to proceed. You'll be dealing with a marketplace and technologies that are constantly evolving.

You'll need to be aware of not just the LMS, but also the quality of the content it houses. I have worked with organizations whose main problem is that no one can find anything in their LMS. So they get a new LMS and then migrate and reorganize the content to make it easier for people to find relevant courses easily and quickly. A big success, right? Not if the content is bad. Making content easier to find may just expose the fact that much of it is boring, inaccurate, out of date, or no longer relevant. So, it will be very important for you to inventory and curate your content and take the opportunity to retire and update it as appropriate, in tandem with your LMS initiative.

Key Takeaways

This chapter introduced the learning and performance ecosystem concept and described the LMS role within the broader ecosystem model. The key takeaways are:

- Training is not the only way people learn. We also learn through practicing and gaining experience, using tools and resources, completing self-directed study and research, observing and networking with others, and consulting with experts.
- Academic education programs are becoming increasingly experiential. Corporate L&D organizations are shifting from a focus on learning to a focus on job performance and productivity.
- Learning and performance ecosystem solutions can consist of any combination of performance support, knowledge management, access to experts, social networking and collaboration, structured learning, and talent management.
- In the learning and performance ecosystem, our role is not just to teach, but to create environments where people can learn on their own and from one another.
- Learning and performance ecosystems allow us to measure the impact of our solutions using productivity metrics that are most relevant to our sponsors.
- The learning and performance ecosystem is supported by multiple learning technology platforms, some of which may have been deployed by IT and HR but can be used by L&D.
- While the LMS may not be the central, most important technology supporting the learning and performance ecosystem, it is still a critical component.
- Much of the LMS selection, implementation, and operation guidance in this book can be applied to other technology projects as you continue to expand your learning technology tool set.

This book has presented proven practices associated with successful LMS selection and implementation. It has addressed the key technological and operational concerns that you, your project team, and your organization will face during implementation. And it has provided guidance on establishing standards, processes, policies, and governance to continue to get the most from you LMS once it is operational. It's a lot of work, but the benefits of a successful LMS project can be well worth the effort.

Finally, remember that every LMS project is different. Business conditions, technologies, culture, funding, leadership expectations, and time constraints combine to make each effort unique. So before you spend a dime on any product or technology, get all your stakeholders together to discuss what they want to accomplish and arrive at a shared vision. Then take that vision and make it happen.

APPENDIX A

Key Takeaways From Each Chapter

Chapter 1

- An LMS is a multiuser software application, usually accessed through a web browser that helps organizations manage training events, self-paced courses, and blended learning programs.
- The three main categories of LMS products are corporate LMS, academic LMS, and integrated LCMS-LMS. Each has a unique feature set and use model.
- There are commercial and open source LMS products. A commercial LMS is fully supported by the manufacturer; an open source LMS has no licensing costs.
- Most LMS products are stand-alone systems. However, some are packaged as apps or plug-ins for popular website frameworks such as WordPress, SharePoint, and Salesforce.
- An LMS should not be confused with an LRS, which collects and stores xAPI learning data generated in other systems. While LMS users are learners, instructors, and learning administrators, LRS users are xAPI developers and data analysts.

Chapter 2

- A corporate LMS is used to deliver learning programs to employees and, in some cases, to customers and business partners.
- Corporate LMS products offer features for managing users, courses, and user-course interactions.
- Corporate LMS products provide features for system administration and reporting.
- Some products offer messaging and discussions, e-commerce, competency management, and other features.

Chapter 3

- An academic LMS is used as a virtual classroom environment to replace or augment a physical classroom.
- Academic LMS products are used by a wide variety of organizations, including higher education, continuous adult education, government, and professional associations. Businesses sometimes use an academic LMS in combination with a corporate LMS.
- Academic LMS products offer features for managing users and course content.
- Academic LMS products provide features for class administration and reporting.

Chapter 4

- An LCMS-LMS has collaborative course development tools and delivery features.
- LCMS-LMS products are mostly used by organizations that develop and deliver their own learning content.
- LCMS-LMS course development features support collaborative authoring, a searchable content library, version control, global changes, templates and skins, reusable content, development workflows, and exporting content to different formats.

Chapter 5

- Three corporate LMS interoperability specifications ensure your e-learning courseware works properly with your LMS: AICC, SCORM, and cmi5.
- A collection of academic LMS interoperability specifications ensures your online content, teaching tools, and LMS can exchange data: Learning Tools

Interoperability®, Question & Test Interoperability®, OneRoster®, Learning Information Services®, Common Cartridge®, Thin Common Cartridge®, Caliper Analytics®, and Open Badges.

- Three standards support data sharing among the various learning technologies, including the LMS, used in business, government, and professional associations: the xAPI specification, the Competency and Skills System, and the vision for a total learning architecture.
- Accessibility standards like Web Content Accessibility Guidelines and Section 508 work with assistive devices to make software applications usable to more people with visual, physical, auditory, and cognitive challenges.
- Security and data privacy are concerns for any information system, including your LMS.

Chapter 6

- A thorough needs analysis engages stakeholders and sponsors throughout your organization to identify your learning management system needs. Make sure to explore the viewpoints of your executive leadership, management, and IT.
- Clearly define and document your requirements and use them as the basis of your product selection criteria.
- Derive vetting criteria from your requirements; that is, distinctive requirements that will help you select a short list of vendors to evaluate.
- A funnel approach to your product evaluation activities helps you narrow hundreds of products down to the handful that are best matched to your requirements.
- Getting bids from two or three vendors whose products are equally good candidates for your organization positions you to negotiate the best terms and pricing.

Chapter 7

- A core team will have primary responsibility for the success of the implementation, and an extended team will be involved in several of the more resource-intensive implementation tasks, like user acceptance testing.
- Implementation of an LMS hosted on-premise can take six to 12 months. Implementation of an LMS in the cloud can take three to nine months. If your

requirements were not well defined and your system is not well suited to your organization's needs, the implementation is likely to take much longer.

- Planning is rigorous at the beginning of the implementation process, and it continues all the way up to the day on which your system goes live. A strong project manager is a key asset to your core team.
- There are many configuration decisions to make as you implement your LMS, such as authentication, profiles, organizational structure, domains and audiences, security roles and permissions, course catalog, metadata, courses structures, credit types, evaluations, notifications, reports, e-commerce, branding, and homepage layout.

Chapter 8

- LMS products are often integrated with systems that manage user accounts and profiles such as the human resource management system used by a business, the member management system used by a professional association, or the student information system used by an academic institution.
- Implementing a single sign-on solution streamlines the user experience for people who have already logged in to the organization's network, allowing their login credentials to be passed to the LMS automatically so that they do not need to log in again.
- LMS products may also be integrated with portals, enterprise search tools, a company's general ledger, or a data warehouse.
- There are many ways to integrate LMS systems, including data feeds, application programmer interfaces, and deep links to specific LMS webpages.
- When replacing an old LMS with a new one, the training data from the old system must be migrated to the new LMS. This process must be done sequentially and repeated in three different stages.
- A guiding principle is to move as little data as possible to reduce risk and speed the implementation process.
- To migrate data from your old LMS to your new one, you will need to create a map of the data fields across the two systems and compensate for differences in field types, character lengths, and data integrity rules.

- Moving standards-based e-learning courseware can be tricky and must be coordinated with the training data migration process. Different procedures are required to move SCORM, AICC, and cmi5 courseware.

Chapter 9

- User acceptance testing involves thorough end-to-end testing of all LMS learner and administrator features. This is where you, the customer, make sure the LMS is configured, loaded, and operating exactly the way you expect—before you go live!
- There are a number of things you must do to plan your user acceptance testing efforts, including identifying and documenting test cases, preparing testing worksheets, scheduling the tests, and assigning people to perform them.
- As your organization executes the user acceptance testing process, you will need to meet at the end of each day to inventory, document, prioritize, and route bugs that are found. You can create your own bug-tracking spreadsheets or use a commercial bug-management system.
- You must update the status of bugs as they are reported and fixed. Even after a bug is declared "fixed," you must be sure it is retested and the fix is confirmed. You may also need to rerun some of your test cases to make sure that fixing one bug didn't introduce other bugs.
- Going live involves some critical steps that must happen in a prescribed sequence. You will need to work with your team to anticipate things that might go wrong and how to mitigate them.
- You must prepare your users, administrators, and help desk in advance of going live.

Chapter 10

- Standards are a critical ingredient in making an LMS easy to use and administer, yet too many organizations operate without them.
- At a minimum, you need four key policies: content inclusion, content ownership, content life-cycle management, and training data retention.
- Clearly documented and communicated administrative procedures help ensure that learning is managed in a methodical way, consistent with the standards and policies.

- Guidelines and conventions for course titles and course numbers make it easier for people to find relevant content, by avoiding inconsistency, redundancy, and ambiguity.
- With multiple administrators, a common set of standards for configuring learning programs makes the LMS easier to use.
- The LMS taxonomy organizes the content and includes the course catalog menu structure, course metadata tags that enhance searching and reporting, and user profile data used to create course audiences.
- It is important to document your current LMS configuration, along with reasons for your configuration decisions, and keep it up-to-date to inform future changes.
- Implementing a major LMS upgrade or new LMS presents opportunities to clean up your data.
- Governance is critical to your ongoing LMS operations. There is a general model for a governance structure that you can use as a starting point in establishing your own.

Chapter 11

- Look for the LMS to move from the most important L&D technology to being one system among many.
- Look for the LMS to update learner transcripts and issue credits for learning that happens outside the LMS, functioning as a transcript warehouse.
- Look for the LMS to become increasingly "unwrapped" so that its content and functionality can be plugged into existing portals and websites.
- Look for more commercial LMS products to introduce gamification features such as points, badges, and leaderboards.
- Look for the LMS to get much better at what it already does pretty well, shifting from SCORM to cmi5, offering better mobile user interfaces, becoming more streamlined and easier for administrators to use, and offering enhanced search capabilities and personalized dashboards.
- While its feature set grows, the price of the LMS will drop as more open source and low-cost products continue to enter the market.
- There are two types of systems related to the LMS: MOOC delivery systems and microlearning delivery systems.

Chapter 12

- Training is not the only way people learn. We also learn through gaining experience and practice, using tools and resources, completing self-directed study and research, observing and networking with others, and consulting with experts.
- Academic education programs are becoming increasingly experiential. Corporate L&D organizations are shifting from a focus on learning to a focus on job performance and productivity.
- Learning and performance ecosystem solutions can consist of any combination of performance support, knowledge management, access to experts, social networking and collaboration, structured learning, and talent management.
- In the learning and performance ecosystem, our role is not just to teach, but to create environments where people can learn on their own, and from one another.
- The learning and performance ecosystem is supported by multiple learning technology platforms, some of which may have been deployed by IT and HR but can be used by L&D.
- While the LMS may not be the central, most important technology supporting the learning and performance ecosystem, it is still a critical component.
- Much of the LMS selection, implementation, and operation guidance in this book can be applied to other technology projects as you continue to expand your learning technology tool set.

APPENDIX B

Glossary of IT Technical Jargon

Accessibility	The features that allow the LMS to operate in conjunction with assistive devices such as screen readers, voice control, and switch controls so that they can be used by people with visual, physical, auditory, and cognitive challenges.
AD or ADFS	Active Directory or Active Directory Federation Services. Microsoft's single sign-on solution. (See ***Single Sign-On***.)
API	Application programming interface. A library of programming functions allowing software developers to access LMS content and features to integrate it with other systems and applications or automate manual tasks and processes.
Backups	A scheduled set of processes that pull data from the LMS servers and store them for retrieval in the event that the server's data is overwritten or lost.
Configuration Management	A methodical approach to implementing changes to the configurable settings of an LMS.
CSV	Comma separated values. One of several file formats (.csv) for data feeds that can be viewed and edited using spreadsheet software such as Microsoft Excel.

Dashboard	A high-level graphical view of multiple types of data tracked in an LMS that is typically displayed as pie, bar, or cluster charts; heat maps; or other formats.
Data Feed	A type of integration between two information systems where data are automatically extracted from the source system and loaded into the LMS, usually on a recurring scheduled basis.
Data Migration	The process involved in moving data out of an old LMS and into the new LMS that will replace it.
Day One Support	The problem resolution services that are expected from a help desk on the first day users begin using a new LMS.
Deep Link	A web address to a specific page within the LMS that is one or more hierarchical levels below its homepage.
Disaster Recovery (DR)	A comprehensive plan for recovering from a major event, such as an earthquake, fire, or flood at the data center that renders the primary LMS servers and network permanently incapacitated.
Downtime	The time that elapses when user access to the LMS is disrupted (the opposite of uptime).
Error Log	An automatically generated test file that contains a time-stamped list of all error conditions, codes, and messages that occur while the LMS application is running.
Escalation Process	The conditions and rules under which a reported LMS problem is routed to more highly skilled support staff.
ETL	Extract-transform-load. Another term for a data feed, in which data are automatically extracted from a source system, transformed into a specified format, and loaded into the LMS.
Failover	A solution for transferring LMS data and users to an operational server or network if the primary server or network fails.
GoLive	The date upon which the LMS first becomes accessible to end users.

Help Desk Script	Documentation containing a list of anticipated help desk inquiries, procedures and information to resolve them, and escalation processes for problems that cannot be resolved by help desk staff.
Hosting	The hardware on which the LMS software is installed, the network through which it is accessed, and the performance guarantees and data center services involved in keeping it running and reliable, such as system monitoring, backups, failover, and disaster recovery.
HRMS	Human resource management system. A system that businesses use to manage employee information. Also known as a human resource information system (HRIS).
Instance	A specific installation of the LMS on a server. Two of the most typical instances are staging and production. The staging instance is a limited access installation of the LMS used for testing purposes. The production instance is the main instance, which is available to end users. Can also be referred to as site or environment.
Kerberos	A software protocol for network authentication that can be used in single sign-on solutions.
LDAP	Lightweight Directory Access Protocol. A software protocol for resource location that can be used in a single sign-on solution.
Load Testing	A method for testing LMS software that simulates a configurable number of users accessing the system simultaneously and measures how response time and other aspects of its performance are affected.
Maintenance	Software bug fixes, patches, and minor and major releases to the LMS software.
MMS	Membership management system. A system that professional associations use to manage member information. Also known as an associate management system (AMS).
oAuth	Open authorization. An open standard for authentication and authorization that can be used in single sign-on solutions.
Performance Guarantee	A contractual obligation that specifies the percentage of expected uptime, such as 99.97 percent, outage resolution times, and other speed and reliability parameters for the LMS.

Player	Software that typically plugs into an Internet browser to provide special features that run specific file types. In the LMS context, players may be required for a user to run a SCORM course, video, audio, or a webinar.
Production	The installation or instance of an LMS that contains your most current content and is accessible to end users.
Remote Server	A computer on the network where course content is stored and accessed by users through the LMS. The server is "remote" because it is not the LMS server. The LMS links to the web addresses of courses on the remote server.
Response Time	The amount of elapsed time between a user-triggered action and the LMS application's response.
Responsive	A software application design method that ensures the user interface is rendered appropriately on all devices, screen sizes, and resolutions.
REST	Representational state transfer. A best practice approach to creating well-designed system interfaces and APIs that enable software applications to communicate with one another through the web. REST APIs are sometimes called RESTful.
Rotating Backups	A proven practice in reliable data handling where, for example, daily backups are stored for the last seven days prior to the current date, weekly backups are stored for the last five weeks, monthly backups for the last three months, quarterly backups for the last four quarters, and annual backups for the last seven years.
SAML	Security Assertion Markup Language. An open standard for authentication and authorization that can be used in single sign-on solutions.
Scheduled Process	An automated software process, such as a backup or data feed, that is queued to be run automatically at a specific date and time, which may be recurring.
Server	The computer on which your LMS application is installed. Multiple users can access the LMS by navigating to the web address of the server.
Service-Oriented Architecture (SOA)	An approach to software design where an application supporting a specific business activity is assembled using many discrete components from a variety of vendors and products.

Single Sign-On (SSO)	A method for maintaining the identity of users in a central repository, sometimes called an identity provider, which is available to multiple enterprise systems and applications. After the user has logged in to one SSO-enabled system, they are automatically logged in to any other SSO-enabled system they access. For more information, see: AD, Kerberos, LDAP, oAuth, and SAML.
SIS	Student information system. A system that academic institutions use to manage student information.
SSL	Secure Sockets Layer. A security protocol that encrypts all communications between your LMS and the browser of anyone who accesses it. The address of webpages running under SSL appears as HTTPS, instead of HTTP.
Staging	The installation or instance of the LMS that is used for testing purposes and is only accessible to administrators. After going live, you can use the staging site to try out new configurations, test previously unused features, install and test new e-learning programs, and test new versions of the LMS before making them available in production. Throughout the implementation process leading up to going live, you will be working almost exclusively in staging. Also known as testbed, UAT, or QA.
System Configuration	Every LMS offers a set of properties with values that can be entered or selected by the customer organization. Once configured, these properties determine how the LMS looks and behaves.
System Heartbeat	An indication of whether your LMS server is up and running. Typically monitored around the clock by an automated software program running on a different server on the same network as the LMS, which alerts data center administrators within seconds of a system disruption.
System Monitoring	Monitoring ensures that the LMS servers and network are continuously up, running, and accessible.
Systems Integration	A method by which two systems share data or trigger each other's functionality. Many organizations need the LMS to fit into their broader IT technology infrastructure, which may require one or more systems integrations.
Systems Integration Testing	The process by which systems integrators fully and methodically test all LMS integrations with other systems to ensure that they are working properly.

Tiered Support	A model for LMS support composed of multiple support levels or tiers, which typically include a help desk as the first tier, LMS administrators as the second tier, and IT and the LMS vendor as the third tier.
UAT	User acceptance testing. The process by which your organization (the user) fully and methodically tests all LMS features, functionality, and content to ensure it is working as you expect before you go live.
Uptime	The time that elapses when user access to the LMS is continuous without disruption (the opposite of downtime).
XML	Extensible markup language. One of several file formats (.xml) for data feeds that can be viewed and edited using an XML or HTML editor.

APPENDIX C

Glossary of Terms With Different Meanings for L&D and IT

	L&D Definition	IT Definition
Client	The sponsor who pays for a learning program to be developed and delivered.	The software, such as browser or player, that runs on a user's computer or mobile device that accesses software from a server. When you mention a client, IT may think you are talking about software.
Content	The e-learning courseware that is installed on an LMS.	The data contained in a system. Your IT partners may not understand your distinction between what you refer to as data, which reside in the LMS database, and what you refer to as content, which is the e-learning courseware residing in a file system on the LMS server or a remote file server.

	L&D Definition	**IT Definition**
Domain	A method for segmenting the users, administrators, and content in a single customer's multitenant implementation of an LMS. For example, an organization may have three separately administered domains for employees, customers, and distributors.	The part of the web address (URL) that appears directly after http:// and ends with .com, .org, .edu, .gov, and so on.
Registration	The process of enrolling in a course.	The process of creating a new user account. When you talk about user registrations to IT, they may not understand that you are referring to user enrollments.
Training	The courses that reside in the LMS.	A way to prepare new users of the software.
xAPI	Experience API. A method for tracking learning activity data.	Your IT organization may mistake this to represent your LMS API, which provides programmatic access to LMS functionality. Be sure to explain the difference to them.

References

Berking, P., S. Foreman, J. Haag, and C. Wiggins. 2014. *The Experience API: Liberating Learning Design.* Santa Rosa, CA: The eLearning Guild.

Feldman, S. 2004. "The High Cost of Not Finding Information." *KMWorld* 13(3).

Foreman, S. 2010. "Advanced E-Learning Technology Architecture: Moving Beyond Course Delivery." Presented at the Learning Solutions Conference & Expo, March 24-26, Orlando, FL.

———. 2013a. *Evaluating and Selecting a Learning Management System (LMS).* Santa Rosa, CA: The eLearning Guild.

———. 2013b. "Five Steps to Evaluate and Select an LMS: Proven Practices." *Learning Solutions Magazine,* June 5. www.learningsolutionsmag.com/articles/1181/five-steps-to-evaluate-and-select-an-lms-proven-practices.

———. 2013c. "The Six Proven Steps for Successful LMS Implementation (Part 1 of 2)." *Learning Solutions Magazine,* July 29. www.learningsolutionsmag.com/articles/1214/the-six-proven-steps-for-successful-lms-implementation-part-1-of-2.

———. 2013d. "The Six Proven Steps for Successful LMS Implementation (Part 2 of 2)." *Learning Solutions Magazine,* August 5. www.learningsolutionsmag.com/articles/1217/the-six-proven-steps-for-successful-lms-implementation-part-2-of-2.

———. 2013e. "LMS Operation and Governance: Taming the Beast." *Learning Solutions Magazine,* September 9. www.learningsolutionsmag.com/articles/1244/lms-operation-and-governance-taming-the-beast.

———. 2013f. "The xAPI and the LMS: What Does the Future Hold?" *Learning Solutions Magazine,* October 14. www.learningsolutionsmag.com/articles/1271/the-xapi-and-the-lms-what-does-the-future-hold.

———. 2015. *Learning and Performance Ecosystems: Current State and Challenges.* Santa Rosa, CA: The eLearning Guild.

Gallagher, P.S., J.T. Folsom-Kovarick, S. Schatz, A. Barr, and S. Turkaly. 2017. "Total Learning Architecture Development: A Design-Based Research Approach." Presented at Interservice/Industry Training, Simulation, and Education Conference, Arlington, VA.

MarketsandMarkets. 2016. *Learning Management System Market by Application, Delivery Mode (Distance Learning and Instructor-Led Training), Deployment (On-Premises and Cloud), User Type (Academic and Corporate), Vertical, and Region—Global Forecast to 2021.* Seattle, WA: MarketsandMarkets.

Murray, A.J. 2015. *Deep Learning Manual: The Knowledge Explorer's Guide to Self-Discovery in Education, Work, and Life.* Boyce, VA: Applied Knowledge Sciences Press.

Ostashewski, N., and D. Reid. 2014. "A History and Frameworks of Digital Badges in Education." In *Gamification in Education and Business,* edited by T. Reiners and L. Wood, 187-200. Switzerland: Springer.

Peer 2 Peer University and the Mozilla Foundation. 2011. *An Open Badge System Framework: A Foundational Piece on Assessment and Badges for Open, Informal and Social Learning Environments.* DMLcentral, March 1. https://dml2011.dmlhub.net/node/4440.html.

Rehabilitation Continuing Education Program. 2004. "The Public Mandate: A Federal Overview, Module 1: History of Vocational Rehabilitation." Minnesota Governor's Council on Developmental Disabilities. http://mn.gov/mnddc/parallels2/four/rehab_act/rehab1.html.

Rosenberg, M. 2006. *Beyond E-Learning: Approaches and Technologies to Enhance Organizational Knowledge, Learning, and Performance.* San Francisco: Pfeiffer.

Rosenberg, M., and S. Foreman. 2014. *Learning and Performance Ecosystems: Strategy, Technology, Impact, and Challenges.* Santa Rosa, CA: The eLearning Guild.

Rustici, M. 2009. "SCORM Versions—an eLearning Standards Roadmap." Rustici Software, January 6. https://scorm.com/scorm-explained/business-of-scorm/scorm-versions.

Segrave S., and D. Holt. 2003. "Contemporary Learning Environments: Designing e-Learning for Education in the Professions." *Distance Education* 24(1): 7-24.

Thomas, D., and J.S. Brown. 2011. *A New Culture of Learning: Cultivating the Imagination for a World of Constant Change.* CreateSpace.

Walli, B. 2014 "Taxonomy 101: The Basics and Getting Started With Taxonomies." *KM World,* August 15. www.kmworld.com/Articles/Editorial/What-Is-.../Taxonomy-101-The-Basics-and-Getting-Started-with-Taxonomies-98787.aspx.

Werkenthin, A. 2016. "ADL cmi5 Committee Announces Release of Quartz Version of cmi5 Specification." *Learning Solutions Magazine,* June 1. www.learningsolutionsmag.com/articles/1977/adl-cmi5-committee-announces-release-of-quartz-version-of-cmi5-specification.

About the Author

Steve Foreman is principal at InfoMedia Designs, a management consulting firm focused on the application of technology to support human performance.

Steve regularly works with organizations in the private and public sectors that are selecting and implementing learning management systems. He assists clients in all areas of system implementation, including strategy, technology, process, standards, and governance.

Some of Steve's key interests include learning strategy analysis and development, connecting learning and business metrics, learning and performance ecosystems, learning technology architecture, socially adaptive systems, self-organizing knowledge bases, performance-centered user interface design, computer adaptive testing, inference-based decision support, and the convergence of working and learning.

Index

D

E

F

G

H

I

L